Love is the Healer Death is a Vehicle

by

Susan Gobin

To Deanna
In love & gratitude,
Susan

Love is the Healer

Death is a Vehicle

Author photo by Mary Gottwald

ISBN 1-932196-44-7

WordWright.biz

P.O. Box 1785
Georgetown, TX 78627

Printed in the United States of America

I would like to dedicate this book to
My Father and Mother
And all parents
Whose love and lessons
Have not yet been recognized
Or acknowledged

I would like to offer a special thank you to
Lyn Dickerson and Amy Weidmann for
Continuing to believe that this
Book should be published
And Joan R. Neubauer for doing it

Introduction

The story you are about to read is based on my experience and the experiences of my family through my father's death. My father experienced all of the near-death phenomena that are so popular today, out loud, with him not believing any of it. He was not on any pain medication, and it was verified that he was not oxygen deprived. The essence of this story is that the persistence of God's love, the love of the family, and in retrospect my father's love for us, although it certainly did not seem that way at the time, resulted in healing for him, us and hopefully many more.

After twenty years of working with the dying, I have learned that *healing* does come with *death*, love is what it is all about, and we don't have to wait until it's our turn to die to realize it. *God is love*, and love uses whatever vehicle it takes to get you home.

My generation, the baby boomers, gets closer and closer to our own journey Home. Some of us have already experienced the loss of a parent, spouse, friend, or maybe even a child. The truth, however, is that even if you have been fortunate enough not to, you will. And, eventually it will be our turn. This book is not a "how to" or "self help guide" on death, but more like a documentary on what happens when spirituality is only an idea or concept, rather than part of your everyday life. It is real, and no amount of exercise, nutrition, reading, prayer or meditation will stop the death of the body.

The other thing is that with all the therapy my generation has used, many have divorced themselves from their parents, or decided they had gotten the raw end of the deal when fathers and mothers were handed out. Well, I'm here to tell you that even the "Leave it to Beaver" families produced children that don't know what it means to be themselves, and *all* parents are teachers that deserve our gratitude and love. Maybe we will be able to do for them in their time of need what we think or have been told they didn't do for us.

The Bible tells us to "honor our father and our mother." Buddhists say you can never repay your parents for bringing you into this world. Neither makes a distinction between *good or bad* parents. Mind you, this is coming from someone who as a teenager, continually told her parents she didn't owe them anything because she never asked to be born.

Some of you may wonder why I would put such personal and sometimes disturbing scenes out for everyone to see. Well, if it makes you think or question or explore your long held beliefs, the ones you were taught but never experienced, the ones you say you believe but can't find when things seem to be falling apart, I will have done one of the jobs my God requires of me.

Chapter 1

The Call

February 26, 1995

My mom called and said they'd put my father in the hospital again. She felt I should come to San Antonio right away. I left my home in Austin and arriving at the hospital ninety minutes later, found an empty room, clean and made up. My heart fell. I found a nurse who told me they had taken him to a different floor to stabilize him. Later, he'd return to a palliative care floor, where they would provide only comfort care while he prepared to die. The nurses, not my mom, told me this. I went to find my parents.

For four years Daddy suffered from a rare autoimmune disease called polyarteritis nodosa, in which the inflammation of the arteries eventually shuts down the organs. Until recently, this disease usually caused death within a year, but because of advances in treatment, Daddy stayed with us a while.

After what I just learned, I couldn't go home. I decided to stay at the hospital. My mom and I spent the night in the room with Daddy, every night until we took him home March 3. That began a six-week intensive course in love, reconciliation, pain, transition, and ultimately transformation for my family. I have no doubt that my dad and I had a working contract or destiny, whatever you want to call it, in place long before 1995. Hopefully, it will help others.

When I started school at age 5½, I lived in terror that my father would go to hell for not going to Mass on Sunday, for eating meat on Friday, and many other awful things. I constantly prayed, making spiritual bouquets, and placing "miraculous medals" under his mattress. I did this until I reached age 12 or 13. Strangely, I didn't worry about the rest of my family: mother, grandmothers, sister or anyone else, even though they did exactly what my Daddy did. I guess I knew they'd survive, although I didn't know why. (Did I mention I was raised Catholic?)

My faith made more of an impression on me than on others, and nuns from the first grade through high school reinforced my heartfelt belief that I had a vocation, a calling, and for them this meant my destiny was the convent.

Before school when my grandmother took me shopping at Joske's, "The Store" downtown, I threw fits to go into St. Joseph's Church next door. There I'd gaze at the life-size statues of the crucifixion and a scene where they took Jesus off the cross and laid him in the arms of his mother. This mesmerized me.

Although my parents sent me to a Catholic school, they refused to hear me talk about entering the convent after eighth grade. My focus changed. Rather than listening to everyone else, I listened to me and only me. I did not even listen to God, at least not consciously. More than thirty years later, as daddy approached his final months of life, I found myself again completely terrified of losing my father to darkness unless I could help him. Although my whole concept of life after death, and why I thought I'd lose him, changed dramatically, my father remained the same. He feared hell but consciously refused to talk about God or death, denying, as he had in life, their very existence.

I realize we all have a purpose, a calling. that no one else can fulfill. We all fill a certain niche, form one piece of the puzzle, the big picture, but until now my belief seemed nebulous. Now I realized the reality. It is physical. A case of semantics, maybe, but it's true. God exists; God doesn't exist; there is a hell but there isn't a hell; there is sin but there isn't; there is creation and there is evolution, and, most important, the only opposite of love is fear.

My family proves this. I see that if Daddy had been as happy and loving and supportive as I had always wanted, neither my purpose nor this story would exist. God has a plan.

I write this recognizing that my family may not understand that we get to the light only by acknowledging the dark. Unpleasant and uncomfortable parts of this story ultimately make it beautiful. I write this because I feel called to write it for you. If we exist as one, then you need this information as much as I did, as much as my Daddy did. All of us will die. Not any of us gets out any other way. Even Jesus died before he could prove the existence of life beyond the grave. Wouldn't you like a road map? I have no credentials, no degrees, simply the step-by-step experiences of my life and my continual search for truth that has brought me to this moment. You don't have to believe it, but I present the truth as I experienced it. Others in my family have a different perspective, but the facts remain the same. Only our interpretations differ, and I know that Daddy did what he did for all of us.

In a book my mother wrote for the family she said that I brought her religion. Although I walk a long road, I hope to bring you a living example of a personal, all-loving God who completed His work and waits on us to do ours, giving us all the support and help we need, all for the asking. The bigger message and the oldest, is one of love. Regardless of the circumstances, God is love, and all people can experience it. I believe the importance of this story lies in the fact that we are ordinary, everyday people.

Chapter 2

A Brief History of the Players

A young Irish woman of 21 gave birth to my father, Walter, September 26, 1919, in San Antonio. She and her German husband raised two children. Walter came first. His sister, Barbara Jean, arrived almost six years later. My grandmother never worked outside the home, and my grandfather was first a salesman and then a successful lawyer. My grandmother told me most of the childhood stories about Daddy. She said her son always loved animals. His pets included guinea pigs, turtles, etc. As he grew older he added a donkey, and even acquired a horse used in the movies.

Walter took risks as a child, and always had a temper. My grandmother talked about him running and butting his head into the wall at age two and knocking himself down. He did that over and over until she lay down on the bed and cried. He must have wanted to know his pain could make a difference. Then he stopped. Other family members' stories implied he was an unhappy teenager, but I don't know why. I do know that my grandparents lived their own lives and partied a lot. Although they lived in a middle class home in a middle class neighborhood, my grandfather showered my grandmother with diamonds, furs and a Cadillac. I never realized until now how ahead of its time that Cadillac was. Made in 1949, it featured all power windows, pushbutton ignition and many other extras. I sat on the armrest in the front seat between them. I must have been quite small, but as I remember it I sat on a throne and they loved me very much. I sometimes wonder if they gave my father or his sister that same kind of love and nurturing that they so easily bestowed on me.

My father was a good man, faithful to his wife for almost 50 years. He did not cheat or steal. He wasn't a drunk. He provided well for his family. He never tried to hurt anyone out of the family, although he never went out of his way to help anyone outside the family either. He just didn't know how to express his love within the family. Moreover, I don't believe he felt like anyone really loved him. He spent lots of time with us as kids, a lot more than mom, but teased us more than he showed affection. Over the years whenever I gave him a present he usually said, "What did you do that for? I don't want or need that." One time I even remember turning around right then and there and taking it back to the store. I gave him a record by a piano player I thought he liked. I wanted to thrill him.

He prided himself on teaching us different breeds of animals and about plants we saw on our Sunday afternoon car rides, a ritual that continued even after I left home. We'd go to the zoo and the amusement park probably once a month. He did not bestow much affection, although more than Mama did. I don't ever remember seeing him and Mama show affection to each other either.

I don't have any idea what really caused all my Daddy's pain, because he denied he had any, but he often embarrassed me to the point of utter shame and humiliation. He was very protective of us. Through high school I wasn't allowed to date. It never seemed to me that he worried what boys might want to do with me, but more what I might try to do with them. He often told me how bad women were. When I turned 18 I got drunk on a New Year's Eve date because my boyfriend told me he didn't love me anymore. Daddy took me out to drive his car the next day, (I wasn't usually allowed to drive).

He kept telling me to go faster and faster and then said, "The next concrete pillar we come to, I want you to drive straight into it, because you don't deserve to live, and I don't want to anymore."

I don't remember freaking out or anything, just slowing the car back down and turning around and going home. What kept me from doing it? I had already attempted suicide at 14, although he didn't know about it. I believe God and His grace saved me. How could my actions affect him so? What about his relationship with Mama and my sister, Debbie? Was I that important? Something connected Daddy and me.

My mother, Alice, was born March 26, 1923, the youngest of five children, one boy and four girls. Her brother, Johnny, died in his twenties from internal bleeding. After reading some of her accounts of his death, I believe part of her stopped feeling then. She said that at his funeral she remembered feeling really weak and almost fainting or falling down because the loss overwhelmed her. Her father told her to control herself, stand up, and never give in. She said she never felt the same.

She remains very independent, but I don't think she recognizes it. She worked for the telephone company as a management secretary when I was growing up, and often told me mothering was not her strong point. She and Daddy both wanted the best education for us and therefore sent me to private schools all the way through high school, even though we lived in a one-bedroom apartment until I turned twelve. She never doubted her way was the right way. Now I know she did everything the best way she knew how.

Mama and Daddy knew each other as children. They lived in the same neighborhood, right around the corner from each other. Mama said they got married because they felt comfortable with each other and because everyone they knew was getting married. She feared the *old maid* label. Approximately three months after the wedding they found out I'd arrive soon after their first anniversary.

Mama worked and my grandmother took care of me almost all the time. At some point Daddy started to go to law school, but decided to go the more secure route of civil service. My mother needed security and a no risk environment. I don't ever remember Dad happy about work. Whenever the phone rang, he instructed us to say he wasn't home. Oddly enough, everyone, employees and friends, loved my Daddy's company, even though he didn't feel the same way. He took early disability retirement at age 55, called himself old, and then stayed home just waiting for the end except for those Sunday rides, which at this point increased in frequency. After my grandmother (his mother) died in 1985, he turned even more despondent.

I was born October 1, 1946, one of the first of the baby boomers. My Daddy's parents treated me, their first grandchild, like a princess. As I said before, I surprised my parents, and not pleasantly. They knew me as sensitive, intelligent, and possessed of a strong desire to please. Schoolmates knew me as teacher's pet, and the star of all the school plays through junior high. In the first grade alone, I played Mary in the Christmas pageant, as well as Cinderella. Along with playing dress up, dancing girls and horses (I was the king of the wild horses), I forever made altars with statues and flowers and tried to convince my sister and girlfriends to come pray with me. I understand now why no one took me up on it.

As an impressionable child, I believed every word the nuns said. Even though my family was Catholic, Daddy challenged me on every piece of dogma I learned. I remember standing in line at a Luby's cafeteria arguing about Creation versus Evolution, and not comprehending his argument. (He took the side of evolution.)

He talked about hypnosis, the art of acupuncture, the book about Bridie Murphy and reincarnation, and hearing his father's voice over headphones in an airplane when his dad died saying, "It was easy, Walt, it was easy."

Daddy's temper scared me through elementary school, which made life difficult since I loved him so much. In high school I began to stand up to him and my life got more difficult then. We showed like minds and tempers, but I looked at the world differently. I did not buy his philosophy of life. I spent one year in college; got pregnant; got married; gave birth to three children (Lysa, Rebecca and John); got divorced; went crazy. I remarried a man, Jim, whom God gave to me. I let God and Jim put me back together, and here I am.

My sister, Debbie came along in 1951, and my Mom favored her. According to Mama's own written words, Debbie taught her the meaning of love and what missing someone felt like. Debbie was always fun, and we grew up pretty close. She still tells me she believed in Santa Claus only because I said I saw him. To this day I know exactly where I was when I imagined what I told her I saw, Santa in his sleigh flying to my grandmother's house.

We fought like all siblings do, but we never let anybody else talk about or hurt the other one. While I believed everything the nuns taught, Debbie bought none of it. I think that freed her up to really live her life, and not overanalyze everything like me. That also endeared her to Mama because she didn't really question. During my first marriage and the birth of my children, I was Susie Suburbia. Debbie went wild. When I got divorced we spent some time together sort of transitioning, then she remarried and settled down. I got really wild before I remarried. We feel closer than ever now. She still has the best sense of humor in the family.

My sister Kristina came along a year after my oldest daughter Lysa. My mom stayed home with her, and Daddy retired while she was still little, so she had both parents home most of her life. She did everything my sister Debbie and I didn't do. We did well in school, but she did what they wanted her to do, and more. She joined the pep squad in high school and made pep squad president in her sophomore year. These were things Mama wanted for me but told me I couldn't do because I didn't have rhythm, couldn't dance, and so forth. The difference between Kristy and me was I believed Mama and she showed Mama. She graduated from college with a degree in education, something else I planned to do. She is an outstanding teacher, and during Dad's illness she got her master's degree with awards and accolades. I finally got to know her during our Dad's transition.

My first husband, Charlie, gave me three wonderful children. Lysa, my first, taught me how to be a mother, as I mothered her and as I have watched her mother my four grandchildren. Rebecca most resembles me in everything she is and does. John, the youngest, I feel the most responsible for and connected to by an almost unconscious kind of love, a feeling not unlike what I felt for my Dad. They turned into unique and beautiful individuals and I feel so thankful for the relationship I have with all of them in spite of our early years.

Other people who influenced my life, and have a definite bearing on this story include the many, many friends that I made during my post-divorce years. Many of them are gay, and many of them are dead. I feel close to those still here, as well as those who have gone on. These men supported me when I felt I had no one because I got a divorce. The Church said I'd go to hell, and I didn't know how to fix it. My friends encouraged me always, and a special bond joined us. I didn't fit in this world, and neither did they. Consequently we laughed and partied and loved until we said good-bye. They taught me about life and love in a way that most people just don't understand. They still do. They prepared me for my father's death. They gave me the honor of helping them through their times of need and their transitions, and thus gave me the foundation I needed, strong and indestructible.

Two friends demonstrated the different ends of the spectrum: Michael, who died in 1992, and showed me that when you do not fear, and investigate the process of death beforehand, it can be peaceful, easy and conscious. After a long battle with AIDS he went into the hospital on a Monday afternoon feeling just a little out of sorts, but running a fever. He was pretty fragile and they wanted to check it out. When I went to visit that evening I knew death was near. I really don't know how I knew. He still tried to make small talk, and when I asked him, "Michael, you do know what is going on, don't you?" He replied, "We'll talk about it tomorrow." End of conversation. I stayed until around 2 a.m. and came back about 7 a.m. An old girlfriend of his from school and I stood on either side of the bed. He didn't talk anymore. He required no pain medication at that time, and very slowly and peacefully just stopped breathing about 9 a.m. Up and around on Monday, and gone Tuesday morning. He knew the future and did not fight it.

Danny, a very good friend of Michael's, died in March of 1993. He fought and denied even unto death itself. A friend and I stood by the bed as he died. We all felt his agony. Four days of saying goodbye to family and friends and still he claimed he felt fine. He once said, “Susan, I know everyone says I’m dying, but I don’t even feel sick.” He said this while he could not eat, and had a double IV line in his chest, and a catheter. He took enough medication to kill an elephant. We injected per doctor’s orders, Valium and Dilaudid. Danny blinked when we gave him his medication and then talked for hours. For the last three nights I lay in the bed with him, and we had the most profound conversations ever between midnight and four in the morning. I know that the veil between the worlds gets very thin during transition. He kept insisting on suicide. Then one night as he seemed to sleep, I tried to convince him not to fight it so much, to just let go. I said, “Danny, you’re going to be so surprised at how easy and wonderful it will be.” I looked over at his chest and he was shooting me the finger and smiling. No matter how holy the moment, you had to have a sense of humor.

As an additional gift, I met my husband through these friends. God does work in mysterious ways.

Chapter 3

You Can't Rush the Process

Mom and I got up and down with Daddy all that first night at the hospital. We sat him up. We lay him down. We got him a drink. We did something every fifteen to twenty minutes. Whenever he got comfortable and started to relax, he started to feel like he was slipping away and wanted to sit up. This happens with many people afraid to die. The dying don't necessarily need to sleep, but their caretakers do.

He kept asking, "What's going to happen and why can't the stupid doctors do anything? Don't they know anything? After all, I don't have cancer."

In Daddy's mind, no one died unless he had cancer. Mama wasn't ready to hear that he was dying, and Daddy sure didn't want to.

When the doctor came the next morning I asked lots of questions. I had worked with dying people since 1985 because so many of my friends succumbed to AIDS. But I never feared death, feared talking about it or feared being around it. My grandmother, the one who took me shopping, told me when I was three I gave her more comfort than anyone else when my grandfather died by telling her where I saw him and that he was fishing on a beautiful lake, something Pop had always enjoyed. I wish I could do that now. Anyway, most of the people I associated with knew the words that surround these situations even when they refused to accept the circumstances. Most people with AIDS took "on-the-job training," so to speak, and accepted responsibility for their own care.

My parents did not understand this process. My mother didn't like the questions; my father did not comment. Mama said I wanted Daddy to die, and that I was trying to rush him. She said I shouldn't ask so many questions, and that if I wanted to stay and help, I needed to do just what she told me, not talk to Daddy about any of this. Of course all this happened in front of him.

She said this was "My party and I'm running the show."

I said, "If it's anybody's *party,* I think it's Daddy's."

She asked me to leave, and not politely.

I felt crushed. My mother was too. Did I feel called to do this? My daddy's incredible hardheaded mind needed me to help him through this. I knew it. I called Jim in tears. He asked if he should come get me. I said no, that I just needed to hear a friendly voice.

The next day Mama asked if she could pay me to stay and help. I should do what she said and only that. I told her she couldn't pay me, that I wanted to stay. He was my father. She said that's why money existed, for convenience, and that she really needed me. I couldn't believe she said that—she needed me. I think she said she loved me too. Anyway, a healing took place and I sat on the floor with my head in her lap, crying, saying how I had waited all my life to hear that. She couldn't believe that I didn't feel like she loved me. Our battle was far from over.

Right then, I felt totally okay with death. Looking at it from only our conscious mind and bodily consequences, I thought assisted suicide or euthanasia okay. One evening when my sister Debbie and I went out to dinner I shared a newspaper article by Marian Winik, an Austin author, which very romantically described how her husband, who had AIDS, took his own life. "Why can't Daddy be this thoughtful?" I asked.

She assured me that if she were dying she wanted me there. I confidently pledged to do so. My, how things change. After what Daddy taught me, I could never, ever, suggest such a thing again.

During this week I also began a new relationship with my youngest sister, Kristina. Since she came after I married and had my own family, I didn't get to know her very well as she grew up. Anyway, during the hospital stay, she took me to her house to shower a couple of times, and on one of those occasions gave me a tape that her counselor had given her on death and dying. Gay Luce, a nationally known spiritual teacher who conducts mystery schools everywhere, recorded it. A mystery school delves into the mystical aspects of ancient cultures and religions, and provides experiences of those rituals.

The tape talked of the Egyptians training special people that helped the dying make an easier transition. They accompanied the person and understood the happenings of the afterlife, and more importantly what happened on a physical level. Strikingly, she said the Egyptians felt the spirit leaves the body through the top of the head during a natural death. The Tibetan book of the Dead says the same thing. Luce suggested stroking the head to soothe and comfort the dying person, and to breathe in sync with him.

Dannion Brinkley, author of *Saved by the Light*, teaches about breathing *with* the dying also. They suggested other things, too, but they required the cooperation of the dying. I knew that wasn't going to happen. However, I'd heard and read about the soul leaving through the head and had been privileged to attend the deaths of others.

Strangely, Kristina did not advocate any of this, but opened up enough to bring the tape to me. As it turned out, it was a great gift. Mama always compared Kristy to me, and usually not in a very complimentary way. Whenever she spoke her mind or showed her temper, Mama told her, "You're just like Susan."

Back to the hospital. With Mama in the room, I kept my mouth pretty well closed, but when she left to shower or run errands I talked to Daddy a lot about my thoughts on death. I reminded him of when he heard my grandfather's voice over the headphones in an airplane in 1950, shortly after his fatal heart attack but before anyone had notified him. When Daddy ranted and raved and made racist remarks when watching the news, I told him that when he got to the other side, race might not be so apparent as spirits look different and he wouldn't know the race of those he talked to. He laughed kind of sheepishly and admitted he had better take more care.

I told him I knew he thought I said crazy things, and that I didn't need to talk if he preferred that, but he said I was trying to do the right thing. He really didn't believe any of the ideas in Near Death Experiences (NDEs). Nor did he believe in a light at the end of a tunnel. In fact I'm pretty sure he and Mama thought of those as New Age beliefs and compared New Age to Satanic ideas, or at least not Christian. Daddy believed in immediate Heaven or Hell, or maybe just dying and waiting until the end of the world for resurrection and judgment. At any rate, when Mama talked to Jim about Daddy's skin cancer surgery, I laid on hands and performed some body work on Daddy. He seemed asleep.

When Mama repeated the doctor's remark: "I'm

going to cut these little devils out of here," Daddy's eyes popped wide open and he said, "What devils, Mama?"

It took a while for us to calm him down and explain that she meant the skin cancers

On Wednesday I asked the doctors if I should go back to Austin or if they thought Daddy might die that week. They thought I should stay and said that if he lived until Friday they planned to send him home with hospice care. Mama really didn't want to take Daddy home at first. The hospital seemed like the safest place. I understood her hesitancy. Getting Mama to accept their decision and to agree to hospice care at home was not easy. The doctors, and moreover, God and his angels must have worked on this because at this point she did not welcome my input.

My husband Jim arrived Thursday and gave me a reprieve from the twilight zone for a few hours. He stayed at a Mariott close to the hospital. We ate dinner, drank a glass of wine, and he rubbed my back for a while. Mama felt scared and anxious about taking Daddy home. Jim and I both thought maybe he would really go to his heavenly home before Friday.

About ten that night I went back to the hospital. Mama went to sleep immediately after I got back and Daddy and I were essentially alone. He appeared calm. Without saying a word, he turned over on his right side, away from me, and got into the fetal position. He looked like a child in prayer, with folded hands. I put both my hands on him—one on the back of his head and one on his lower back and I prayed silently the Unity Prayer of Protection as a mantra:

The Light of God surrounds him
The Love of God enfolds him
The Power of God protects him
The Presence of God watches over him
Wherever he is, God is, and all is well!"

When my mind started to wander, I said a prayer I remembered from a workshop with Ram Dass:

May Daddy dwell in his heart
May he know his true self
May he be free from suffering
May he be at peace.

I started at 10:30 p.m. and did not stop or move my hands until somewhere between 2 and 3 a.m. Mama slept soundly. Thunder crashed around us and lightning brightened the room, but Daddy didn't move from his childlike prayer. He had not stayed so still since I arrived on Sunday. He turned over and I thought his time had come. His breathing slowed and he took longer and longer between breaths. I got the nurse. She too thought death might come soon.

I waited a long while, not knowing whether to wake Mom or not. Finally, I went to her and said

"Mama, Daddy might not wait to go home in the morning" She raised up and said, " I thought that might happen" and lay down again. I couldn't believe it! What happened to "It's my party"? I talked to her again, but Mama did not get up. Within minutes Daddy appeared restless again, but so much weaker. His healing had only begun.

Father Jack, the parish priest, came the next morning at Mama's request to give the last rites. Daddy didn't necessarily want him there, but Mama and the priest had quite a social visit at the end of Daddy's bed. She complimented his sermons, how the Church had turned around with him there, and so on. I know she felt nervous and inexperienced but she acted as if Daddy was not there. Then Jim came to help get Daddy home. The doctors gave us a list of what to look for, whom to call, and what to take care with: seizures, fluid build-up around his heart and lungs, and other symptoms. They predicted a short time at home. Mama and I still argued about one thing and another. We both felt the tension, and Jim kept reminding me of how frightened she was.

Just two years earlier, I helped someone in hospice as one of two 24-hour-a-day caretakers. Everybody involved knew what to expect, and still it was very difficult. So this frightened me, too. What if no one mentioned the word "death"?

My parents, married almost 50 years, faced such situations privately. But I never understood why my mother always talked about Daddy as if he weren't there. He was still very conscious, and very Daddy. I saw his frustration, although he never said anything. He, too, felt frightened. Whenever someone asked him a question on any subject, Mother answered. He rolled his eyes or just stared, rather than attempt an answer.

He asked only one question: What if something happened to his heart? Mama didn't want to believe that he was making his last trip, and she said nothing to him about it.

At the hospital, three people helped my dad from the chair to the wheelchair, which sat about 10 inches apart. When we got to the house and parked in the driveway, I remembered Jack Nicholson in *The Shining* as I observed Daddy's soul swooping back into his body. He quickly walked, with a little help, the length of the garage, and took the step up into the house with relative ease. The change appeared immediate and profound. Jim and I stared at each other. You cannot rush the process!

Chapter 4

The Journey Begins Again

Minds and Parachutes Work Best When Open
Bumper sticker

Daddy took charge when he returned home. He asked for cigarettes, told us all what to do, and snapped at all of us. Mama didn't know how the hospice care operated, but they were not supposed to come until Monday. We'd cope with the weekend. I didn't know whether to stay or not. Then Daddy started talking about how nobody knew anything, and that if his heart started acting up that he'd return to the hospital. I reminded him that he wouldn't go back because he couldn't survive surgery. I said Mama and all of us were there for him. He said we could not handle the care taking and he didn't want to hear it. He motioned for me to leave.

I felt hurt, angry, and very tired. So I headed back to Austin, telling Mama to call if she wanted me to come back. She asked Debbie to stay Friday night. She appeared scared, but at least they returned to their own territory.

I cried almost all the way home. How had we gotten so close that week, and then let all our feelings drive us so far apart? I told myself I'd done all that I could. Daddy wouldn't last a week, and he'd die the way he had lived: hardened, scared and alone with Mama in charge. No one could blame me for not helping. I worked for myself and couldn't afford to take off for long anyway. Several of my friends encouraged me to take care of myself and leave well enough alone.

I called Saturday to check in. Mama sounded tired but okay. I still felt exhausted and sore from sleeping in all kinds of strange positions for a week, and often no more than an hour at a time. I visited a massage therapist for a twenty-minute tune-up. She asked the usual questions and I poured out my soul to her. She saved me. She said I'd make the situation easier for all of us if I quit judging.

She hit my blind spot. I said they did not accept his imminent death. I wasn't telling them what to do exactly, just offering them the benefit of my ten years of observing death and knowing that he didn't have to fight it so hard. I knew, although I don't know how, that there is life after death. I read about lots of near-death experiences in books, and listened to many people who had them. I'd had one myself. Inside I knew that it was so. If they only listened to me, Daddy could go peacefully and beautifully and with love. It could be so easy! They fought it, making it so hard, and I wanted to help. I loved my Daddy!

The massage therapist asked if she could give me some advice. I readily agreed. She said, "If they aren't going to change, just do what they want you to do."

She meant I should help Mama with the physical needs and try to keep Daddy happy, even if that meant ignoring death. "If he's happy his last moments, he'll be happy when he gets to the other side," she said, and that sounded good to me.

Suddenly I felt refreshed and ready to go the second mile. In reality, I didn't think clearly. If we hadn't made Daddy happy before, what made me think we could do it now?

I called Mama when I got back to the apartment and said that I'd come down that evening if she still needed help. She answered with gratitude.

I made a tape of Leonard Cohen singing "Always." ("I'll be loving you always, always.") I made it for Daddy because of Cohen's deep voice. I envisioned Mama and Daddy cuddling, and then he'd let go. My mind and heart felt sure that our future held peace and beauty.

Then reality set in. Mama kept reminding me that Daddy didn't want to hear anything about dying, so I decided to talk about the fun things we did years ago, before I started parting ways with him. He laughed some, and then looked somber. I said, “Daddy, even those times that we didn’t have fun taught me so much. I have so much to thank you for.” That night he sat in a chair for the length of the movie “Paper Moon,” with Ryan and Tatum O’Neal. I had never seen it before. It ended about 1 or 2 in the morning, and he smoked and sat quietly until then. He acted as if he knew I wanted to watch it and he didn’t want to interrupt. But at the end he said, quite “Daddylike,” “That was the most stupid movie I’ve ever seen in my life.”

I responded, “You think so, Daddy?”

Then he wanted to go back to the couch.

Mama got some rest those two nights and I felt really close to Daddy. He usually wanted to go into the den about every fifteen minutes, smoke a cigarette, and then return to the sofa. He did not want to go to bed. I guess he thought that meant the end, and he sure didn’t want to fall asleep, although he kept complaining that he wasn’t getting any rest. He couldn’t walk without help and he commented more than once that first evening “how strong” I was. I believe now he was acknowledging more than my physical strength.

On Sunday Mama and I talked some about our family and our lives. She never wanted to discuss the bad times or admit that they had happened. She preferred to believe we lived the perfect life, despite the competition between us, in her mind, about Daddy.

Monday hospice care started. The nurse came, a male nurse named Michael. Daddy refused to look at him. Mama and I both thought he might be gay, which would have made his presence even more difficult for Daddy. He certainly wasn't afraid to say how he felt about that. However, Michael did just fine. He also had a prison ministry downtown. Daddy answered his questions dutifully, but did not offer any extra information. After Michael left, Daddy asked if he was black. He didn't know, since he had not even looked up to see his face.

Mama kept saying that 90 percent of people who died did not reach the peace I talked about, particularly a spiritual peace. Then the attendant, Irene, arrived. She'd help with Daddy's baths, and give Mama some free time during the week. We hit it off immediately and she reassured me that hard truths came easier from strangers than family. We talked about some of the deaths I attended and shared some similar stories. She then reminded me of the biblical quote, "He came unto his own and his own received him not." Somehow that helped remind me that even Jesus couldn't convince his family and friends at first. Why did I think my family would listen to me now, especially since they never showed any interest before?

Everyone truly thought Daddy would let go that week. The nurse made it a point to reinforce that, speaking directly to Daddy. It is so important to address the dying themselves and not have conversations as though they weren't there. The Catholic hospice chaplain, Bonnie, came by and I felt a lot of relief. We shared many beliefs. Mama liked her too, but not as much as she liked Michael. Bonnie turned into my support.

Daddy and I got along great now, as a result of the quality time we spent together the two previous nights. Daddy asked me to stay. He said he wanted me there. Here came the weird energy. Mama insisted she needed only hospice help during the week. If Daddy started to die she promised to call. I told her Daddy asked me to stay. She yelled right in front of everyone, that I could stay, but I would not stay up with him at night. That was her job.

Again, I returned to Austin, crying and hoping that Daddy knew how much I loved him, that the hospice "angels" would help them both, and wondering if I'd ever see him alive again. He looked weak and fragile, and none of us could imagine this continuing for more than a week or two.

During the next few weeks I went to San Antonio on weekends and stayed until Monday afternoon. I usually waited for the hospice rep so I could get a report, and every week they repeated that death could come any time. My mom marked a birthday on a Sunday during this time, and the Daily Word, my morning message to myself, actually said "Happy Birthday!" for its words of the day. Mama went to church that morning and my sister brought over two birthday cards for my Dad to pick from. He always gave my mom at least a card and usually took her out to dinner. He rarely got mushy, but he never let those days go by.

He chose the card he wanted, a cute one with bunnies on it, not the romantic sentimental one. Just like Daddy. He made a real effort to sign it, and wrote his full signature. Debbie and I had a hard time holding ourselves together, considering the energy it required of him. He didn't eat enough to keep a bird alive at that time, but he made a supreme effort to tell mama that he wanted some of her birthday cake. He even ate a few bites of dinner. Was this love?

The next day came and I regretfully headed home. The same questions, hopes, and realizations arose: Is this my last farewell? I want to be there! I want him not to be afraid. I want Mama not to hurt. I want my sisters to know that this parting will only be temporary, that he will be as close as we will accept afterwards, and that Daddy was being healed, both physically and spiritually. He had to accept the fact that all of us need others in our journey on earth to really live. He couldn't do everything for himself, and did not need to feel ashamed, or lacking in modesty or dignity for needing help. I have always wondered how I'd feel if I needed strangers to bathe and dress me. Maybe I'd rather my family did it. The love that I observed everyone expressing, the love that touched him, convinced me it didn't matter. All that mattered was the presence of love.

My mom learned much, too. She had opened up

her house and her heart. To see her rubbing Daddy's feet with cream, or just sitting with him, was something I had not seen in my 48 years. She'd made Daddy her whole life, and she couldn't imagine life without him, and didn't want to.

The week before he died was very hard. Michael, the nurse, thought it would be any day. As Mama moved around the house, back and forth, trying to keep it all together, she mentioned reading the Bible, trying to find something to help her. She said she couldn't find anything to fit this situation. I sat down at the breakfast bar, took a breath and opened it to the perfect verse: Mark 14: 34-36, the agony in the garden, where Jesus prayed that if it be His Father's will to skip this crucifixion, he would really appreciate it, but if not, then not his will, but the Father's be done. I read this passage to her, and she said she couldn't believe that I had done that so easily. God worked with me here. I had no idea what to look for at that moment.

Again, after the weekend Mama wanted me to leave. Once again I left in tears. She said she'd call if anything changed. On Thursday morning she called with her usual mixed message. Michael said Daddy was actively dying. "Come as soon as you can!" she pleaded. Then she said, "Tomorrow or Saturday is fine." As soon as you can, tomorrow or Saturday? I called Jim immediately. I laughed as I asked what he thought she meant. Do I go now? Or do I wait? I got up, studied my morning readings, and prayed. I decided to wait until the weekend. A friend's partner was dying also, so I planned to visit with him and his family and gain as much nurturing from my "family" here as possible before going back to the fire.

My husband and daughter gave me strength. They endured my roller-coaster emotions miraculously. I felt frustrated, not because I was losing my father, because I knew I wasn't, but in my seeming inability to convey how much I loved them both. I wanted to be there for them, in every possible way.

That Friday my friend's mother shared a book with me that anyone involved with the dying process should read. It speaks to learning how to live and what is ultimately important in this life. Two hospice workers named Callanan and Kelly wrote the book, *Final Gifts*. In it they share stories of their patients and the different kinds of reconciliation that may take place during the "nearing death experience."

We can gain so much by listening to those on their way from this life to the next. We learn the importance of letting them have their experience without trying to bring them back into our experiences, and we learn how to help calm them and relate to what is actually happening for them. If anyone doubts an afterlife, reading this book and then experiencing the process should make it real. I bought and read the book on Friday night, and prepared for my last trip, unbeknownst to me, on Saturday afternoon.

Several relatives called to check on me.

Apparently Mama told them I was tense and that she'd had to send me home. I assured them I felt fine. The journey begins . . . again.

When I arrived on Saturday afternoon Mama appeared glad to see me, and as always, I hoped for that "family" I had never known. I brought the book, not really believing that she'd read it, but offering it all the same. As I took my position in the living room with Daddy, Mama sat in the den and did indeed read my gift. She began telling everyone all about it, including my sisters and her friends. That afternoon Mama and I discussed Daddy's sister, Barbara Jean, and how a visit with her could fill in the missing piece in Daddy's story. They were estranged, and since he still felt angry, perhaps this was the reconciliation his higher self sought. I knew that Barbie would want to see him. I also knew that if he did not see her, she'd suffer a more difficult time with his passing. I went to get her. I don't remember if we told him. Mama had asked his permission before and he had refused, so we took on a lot of responsibility.

Mama and I both prayed for a successful encounter. When Barbara Jean went into the living room to visit, Mama and I went out on the patio to wait. A half-hour later Barbie came to get us and said the visit went well. She told Daddy that his little sister was there, and that she loved him. He told her that he loved her too. I took her home. Of course, he wasn't exactly happy with us for surprising him. He spent that night more restfully than the previous weekends, but little did we know what was about to happen.

I have read extensively on death and dying, and stories that point to the consciousness of the afterlife. From *On Death and Dying* by Elizabeth Kubler-Ross, to *Life after Life* by Raymond Moody, Stephen Levine's books, and several "near death experience" books. My favorite is *Saved by the Light* by Dannion Brinkley. All of these seemed to confirm things that I already felt deep in my being.

If one takes the time to reflect, they also correspond and confirm the teachings of Jesus Himself. The other book that figured heavily into my perception of the following experience was *Letters to a Dying Friend* by Anton Grosz. This book is based on the *Tibetan Book of the Dead*, but written so anyone can understand. Most significantly, this book indicates that without our bodies our minds travel freely wherever and whenever they will. As fast as thoughts happen equals the speed we can travel to or away from Paradise. A friend of mine who read this book in '92, after reading "Final Exit," the book on suicide and death with dignity, experienced the most peaceful, conscious, beautiful death I have witnessed.

After he read Grosz' book, he did not speak of suicide again, and he embraced death naturally, with complete dignity and no fear. At that time I still very much believed assisted suicide was okay. It made sense to me to spare someone in horrific pain, or to save the family pain, while recognizing that life did indeed go on. However, after Daddy's experience, I believe life is an incredible gift and to end it on purpose shortchanges the person's physical experience as well as their soul's well being, sort of like dropping out of school right before graduation. I believe most of those who have near death experiences come out of their bodies so fast that they don't have time to argue or think about where they are, and consequently experience the transition in awe. They don't have to argue with their conscious minds.

We rarely hear of anyone who had a negative near death experience, though there are some. Even in the positive ones the life review passes quickly, as if unimportant. No one wants to feel uncomfortable or talk about painful things. Stories of near death experiences are important, not only because they confirm an afterlife and an all-merciful loving being or consciousness after this life, but because they can show us that we don't face Hell because of our mistakes but because of our seemingly conscious choices. God made us the way we are, and He does not intend to punish us for living according to our nature. We do enough punishing of ourselves. He allows us to review everything we've done and then feel exactly how we affected others, without punishment, just feelings. Whom have we loved? Whom have we hurt? Then we can make a choice: Which feelings do we want for eternity? Are we ready to move on, or do we still have things to do?

If we all thought of this every night before we went to sleep, if we saw this as our future, the world would probably turn into a much more loving place. It is all according to God's plan. However, He also does not require that we choose Him. Since I started actually listening with my heart, and reading for myself the words of God, rather than listening to some man in a pulpit, I realized that when we say we were made in the image and likeness of God what a disservice we do ourselves when we continually talk about ourselves as sinners. God gave us that free will, and thus He has given us the right to choose to do what He says or what we want without Him punishing us. He asked us not to eat of the tree of the knowledge of good and evil, warning that we would die. I'm just not sure He could perceive that we wouldn't want to do just what He said to stay in constant touch with Him. That was our doing, and continues to be. Back to the mind. I am almost certain that at least for a while after death, both our minds and personalities continue, and our growth also continues. Dannion Brinkley says that we, as human beings, are the most incredible and wonderful of all the creations, even more wonderful than the angels. Angels do exactly what God created them to do. They watch after us, even help us from beyond. They are messengers from God, but they cannot do anything against our will, nor can they create and recreate like we can, like God can. Nor do they get to experience this earthly life. God gave that gift to man alone, because man was meant to be God's companion, not His subject.

After coming to this conclusion I read something from Edgar Cayce. He said, "Man alone can defy his God". The best example I can think of on a purely physical level is that of parent and child. The child would not be here if not for the parent—the parent raises the child and the child chooses to either follow the parental example or not. In a best-case scenario, when the child grows into adulthood, parent and child enjoy love and friendship comparable to no other: Heaven! If they choose not to follow the good example, or if the parenting was bad, the wound never heals: Hell! When we create without acknowledging the Creator, we make only half a creation. Look how well we do when we try to go it alone.

Chapter 5

The Hundredth Monkey

April 9, 1995

My Dad's higher self knew all along to expect death soon. However, his "monkey mind" (He always called Debbie and me monkeys.) his purely human mind, put up walls to keep this knowledge at bay. My Dad developed an incredible mind, albeit a very closed one. Although the more I think about it, it may not have been his mind that was closed but his heart.

This particular Sunday morning the Daily Word read "Today I begin a journey of spiritual discovery." I read it to Mama and she didn't say much. After she left, I went to Dad and asked to read it to him. He said yes. The passage reads:

"Is there a longing in your soul for this day to be better than any other day you have ever experienced? When you believe it can be, you begin a new journey—a journey in which you leave behind doubt and fear, regrets and guilt, and discover your spiritual nature and power.

"Walk the walk of a triumphant child of God, for this is who you are. Talk a language of "I can" which connects you with the truth of your indwelling strength and ability. Accept the reality of yourself as a spiritual being on a divine quest! Yes, beloved, feel the rush of excitement about your journey. Know that God is your constant companion in your journey of discovery, and you will never lose your way." And the scripture: "Then those who went ahead and those who followed were shouting, Hosanna!" Mark 11:9

And so we are!

Daddy smiled the most beautiful smile I had ever seen. He looked so peaceful, I thought the next steps would come easily, and he'd move in this peaceful acceptance. Not so! Later that afternoon as Mama sat reading Final Gifts, I sat with Dad and thought about all the people who might come to help Daddy from the other side. Debbie and I believed that Mommie, our grandmother, would come, or maybe Pop, his father. But for sure Mommie. After all, Daddy had called Mommie every day of his life. She called him her little boy.

However, during her last few years in the nursing home, Daddy resented her and his sister. He rattled off how he had to take her to the hospital for treatments, park the car, and get the wheelchair. He never took into account Mommie's feelings during this ordeal. He saw only himself and his sacrifice.

He went to see her almost every day, but then complained about that too. When she died, no one consulted Daddy about much of anything. His sister, Barbie, took care of everything. She refused to let Daddy into the house or give him anything. Mommie left everything to her daughter to do with as she saw fit. Daddy did not want to forgive his sister or Mommie for that.

Therefore, I thought we'd find a better choice than Mommie. Then I thought of the person my Dad talked about loving and feeling loved by the most as a little boy: his Grandma Hogan. He always got a faraway look in his eyes, and you could tell he remembered really great things about her. I walked into the other room to tell Mama what had just occurred to me, something I had not thought of in years. When we walked back into the living room, Daddy had his hand up, and a beautiful smile on his face. He said, "Grandma." I stood back, awed. I felt her presence and I refused to interrupt this astounding moment. What had made me think of her anyway?

Mom rushed over and took his hand, and then said, "Are you talking about 'grandma hands,' Daddy?" She then turned to me and explained the name she and Daddy gave his hands since they wrinkled, like when you stay in the tub too long. My mother, like most people, wanted to explain away a spiritual experience. But why? I found the experience comforting, and so real. Sometimes Daddy held up his hands and stared at them for long periods of time. I saw others do the same, much like babies when they "discover" their hands and feet, wide-eyed and curious. For both babies and the dying, it appears as though their soul can't figure out its purpose in this body. Like, "What is this?" Why am I in here?"

That night we all got a relatively good night's rest, considering what would happen next. The next morning as Mama sat with Daddy, he started talking to lots of people we couldn't see. He didn't seem disturbed by it at all, and Mama didn't interrupt. She just sat there, reading I think. I watched in amazement. He smiled and laughed, a laugh I had never heard, and said, "Oh, it's so good to see you again, it's been a long time" or "Oh, I don't think I remember you. What happened to that ex-wife of yours?"

He looked like a man in a receiving line at a party, and he seemed to visit with lots of old friends. Most of his friends had passed on in the last few years, but he even laughed and talked with my Uncle Jimmie, who I never thought of as his close friend. He did not seem upset, but quite the contrary, more relaxed and more social and happier to see people than I ever remember. Unable to get up, walk or even sip water from a straw, but he talked and laughed out loud!

This went on for an hour or so, and then he got quiet. He asked us to close the curtains and turn off the light because it was too bright. He made that comment over and over, even though we made the room very dark. Mama put a washcloth on his head because he felt hot, and kissed him on the forehead, and this irritated him. He asked more than once, “Why can’t you see how sensitive my head is?” It seemed like he could not last another 24 hours. But he did, he had work to do. Mama needed to run some errands, but seeing how quickly things moved along, I told her she should ask him if she could leave. He looked frustrated and told her to go ahead. Not five minutes after she left, he said in a very loud voice, “It’s over!”

The hospice aide looked startled, and I wasn’t sure what to do. I told him if he needed to go we’d all be okay, Mama too. I told him how much we all loved him, and how thankful we felt for him. I thought that maybe leaving her was too hard for him, or that maybe she distracted him too much from what he needed to do. I know this sounds cold, but people need to work on their own stuff as needed. I believe interaction with the dying must happen on their turf and not on ours. We should take care of our own issues with the dying long before this process begins.

When Mama returned we told her what transpired and she rushed to his side. “Well, do you have anywhere else to go?” Daddy asked her, sort of irritated. Mama checked with the aide, and after watching Daddy a while decided to call my sisters. They both came prepared to stay the night. When the nurse came he asked Mama if she wanted him to say a prayer with us. Mama agreed and we all gathered around Daddy. Later when I said something about God, Daddy said, "I'm not thinking about that kind of stuff at all."

Sometime in the middle of this mixed up afternoon I felt curious to see if I could feel any energy above the crown of my Daddy's head, per the suggestion in the tape by Gay Luce that my sister Kristi gave me. Daddy rested. If I didn't touch him it shouldn't bother him, should it? More disruptive things occurred around us. As a veteran massage therapist I knew how to feel muscle tension, relaxation and inflammation when I put my hands on a body. But I wasn't good at feeling energy like some body workers can. At least, I didn't think I could. When I placed my left hand about four inches above the top of his head, I felt energy. It felt like a swift, yet soft breeze hitting my hand. It truly frightened me. I wanted to feel it, yet I couldn't believe that I actually did.

I quickly moved my hand back to my side and my father looked at me and said, "Shug, get that monkey cap off my head."

I had no idea what he meant, and asked him. He said I knew what he meant, and to please get the cap off his head. I put my hand back above his head, and he sighed and smiled. I asked if that felt better, and he said that was much better.

I told my sister Kristina that maybe Daddy would be the hundredth monkey for humans and push our collective consciousness over the edge.

I had heard the story of the 100th monkey at a lecture when I worked at a resort/seminar center in 1988. They tell a story of scientists who studied a certain breed of monkeys on an island in the Pacific. They taught one monkey to wash its food, then it taught others. When a certain number of that breed, somewhere around a hundred, started washing their food, all of a sudden all of that breed on other islands started doing it too. I still think Daddy might be it. Did I help him let go a little? I don't know.

Then a series of incredible scenes began. He looked up at the ceiling, absolutely joyful, and exclaimed like a child, "Wow! Wow! Who are you?"

Then he grew angry and said, "Liar, get away," after which he appeared totally disappointed and sort of frightened. This happened maybe five or six times.

After a while he looked like a child at Christmas time, with sparkling eyes, and he asked, "Who are you, Who arrrrrrre you?" And this time he said, loud enough for Mom to hear in the next room, "Bullshit!" Again, he looked like a scolded child.

I thought then, that Jesus Himself spoke to Daddy, because Daddy and I talked many times about whether he'd believe Jesus if He stood at our front door. Now when I think about that moment I imagine Jesus walking away laughing, saying, "Later then. It's up to you."

I might not have said anything if I didn't see so

clearly what was happening. Finally I said, “Daddy, I can’t see what you are seeing, but I do know that whoever is coming to you is coming to help” to which he adamantly said, “I don’t need any help, I’ve never needed any help, why can’t you see this is a set-up and quit screwing with me.” Being the argumentative daughter he had always appreciated before, I said, “Why do you look so afraid and disappointed when they leave, then? Why won’t you go to the light?” To which he responded, “I’ve never been afraid of anything, I’ve already been to the light, and I don’t want to go to the light.” I decided to keep my mouth shut for a while and let someone else sit.

I went into the den with Mama and she asked if I ever saw anyone who had so much trouble dying. I told her that of all the folks I knew, not one fought it so hard. She said she found that hard to believe, seeing as the people I worked with had AIDS. Maybe they prepared more and were exposed to death a lot more than Daddy. I don’t mean they had an easy time, but they did not deny such vivid visions and experiences.

Chapter 6

Our Lives in Review

When Debbie and Kristina arrived they went back to Mama's bedroom. After visiting with them for a while I walked back into the living room with Daddy. He said, "Hello again. Where is the rest of the family, why aren't they at the funeral?" Later that evening Mama and Debbie prepared for bed, Kristina and I planned to take the early shift.

Daddy said, "Shug, come over here and use one of your gimmicks and let me out." When he was in a loving mood, he called me Shug, like when I was very little, and Susan, or any number of other names when he was being the Daddy of the last few years.

Surprised and amused, I felt uncertain about what he meant. After all the times in the last six years that I offered him a massage, now he asked me to use one of my "gimmicks." He said, "You know, let me out."

Kristi stood right beside me. I placed my hand above his head once again. "Like this?" I asked him.

He smiled and said yes. Then he said, "Going out, going out. That's enough. You go to bed." I asked if he wanted us to leave him alone, and he said yes, he needed that. Kristina and I told him good night and said we loved him. He said he loved us, too. Mama came in as we left. I told her Daddy had asked us to be left alone, but she refused. She stayed with him. Debbie already went to bed, and Kristina and I went to separate rooms.

Shortly after that Daddy started moaning, and mumbling. Sometimes it seemed like sobbing. He sometimes said, "Stop! Enough!" and "I didn't know," then, "Stop, please stop!"

This went on all night. I got up once and went into the room with one of my sisters, but I don't remember which one. I focused on Daddy and wanted so much to help. I don't think anybody in that house slept one wink. I remember this as the night from hell. It seemed to me that he reviewed his life, the review that those who have had near death experiences talk about. He'd already seen loved ones, and unearthly beings or angels. He'd traveled to the light and had, at least outwardly, rejected the people and events he did not believe real. These events followed the order of such experiences I heard and read about. However, I hadn't read of another case in which the dying person negated and denied these experiences.

The next morning Kristina and I went to her apartment to rest a little and clean up. She'd endured enough of the craziness, but I just wanted to be there. Debbie left for a while and planned to return later. When I got back, Mama went to take a shower. I lay down on the hospital bed in the living room, parallel to Daddy who still lay on the sofa. He rested quietly then and I thought, *Daddy I don't know if I am making this harder or not, but I just want to help. So I'm giving you every bit of energy I have in my heart, I love you so much and I know we are connected.*

I literally felt an arc of energy going from my heart to his. Just as surely, I felt it stop, as if he had enough and didn't need anymore. For the second time, I felt energy move. This stunned me. Mama came in and I went to bed, exhausted.

Shortly before the nurse arrived my father experienced a release that appeared more than he had demonstrated in weeks. The caretakers worried because he had not had a bowel movement in four days. It took my mom, the nurse and the aide to help.

When the nurse asked my father how he felt that day, Daddy replied, "It's my heart, my heart that is giving me trouble."

He did deal with congestive heart failure, but I believe he spoke from another level when he indicated heart trouble. Besides, he rarely gave so much information to the nurse. For instance, when the nurse asked a week before if Daddy knew where he was, he said, "Well, this sure isn't heaven, I can tell you that."

I believed this marked the beginning of some other

rather miraculous healings. My husband has asked that I not write a whole chapter on bowel movements. Two years ago I'd have agreed and also thought anyone who did so was perverse. However, if body mind and spirit compose us, and work together, I see a direct connection here. Also, my dad remained in complete control and always knew when he needed to relieve himself, and always wanted to get up. He alerted everyone, but not once did he seem embarrassed or modest at this time. When people talk of dignity, and the loss of dignity, they often mean this particular body function. I felt the same when I took care of my dying friends. While I found it easy to care for them, I understood their point of view. I know more now, that it's part of the healing, part of the healing of the body anyway. Once my father's heart filled with love, his body had no room for the darkness and sludge.

For a good part of the afternoon Daddy rested his left hand on an organ, for example, his stomach, liver, or lower abdomen, with his right hand sort of resting off of his body, but up to the side of his head. He said things like, "Wait, wait, okay, I'm ready now." Then he'd place his right hand on his heart for a while. Then, "Okay, that's enough."

None of us knew to whom he talked, but he obviously got instructions from someone. When he took his hand from his heart he'd evacuate again, usually not much, and for sure never as much as the first time. I connected this to his healing. Of course no one in my family wanted to discuss this, but I did take notes, and I did tell my husband and my business partner, who was interested in energy and bodywork. This amazed me. A number of disciplines relate various organs and regions of the body to different emotions and mental attitudes. Louise Hay, in her book "Heal Your Body" explains this in detail, as does Carolyn Myss in several of her books. Then there are the chakras. He touched them all!

Chapter 7

The Battle for Our Souls

I went for a walk that afternoon just to get away. I felt too much energy inside the house. Before I left I had given Daddy some sips of water from the end of a straw. He wasn't able to swallow very much, and weakness prevented him from holding a glass. He didn't want to get up very often anymore. When I got back my mom and my sister sat with him. Daddy sat erect on the couch with his feet on the floor, holding a glass of water and obviously listening to someone at his right side. He smiled and nodded his head, and appeared to be listening to some instructions. He looked at peace with it. I felt awe, and constant observer that I am, stood right in front of him. Mama commented how alive he appeared, how strong, and said he obviously wasn't dying yet. When Daddy looked up, he smiled and handed me the glass of water. He then put out his arms. I asked if he wanted to get up, and he said very unlike him, "No way!" and turned to lie down. I helped him down and he let his legs all the way down and just smiled and smiled very peacefully and closed his eyes. Mama and Debbie said that in my absence he wanted to get up and watch TV. So they had taken him into the den to sit in his recliner, but when he got there he wanted to go back to the sofa. He kept asking for the clicker (the remote) and told them he was tired of watching, and for them to turn the damn thing off. The TV was not on. I can only suppose that he watched something from the other side.

Dannion Brinkley said when he got information about the future he saw it on TV-like screens. As much as Daddy did not like to hear about environmental or disaster stuff, I believe if that's what he saw, it annoyed him and he wanted to turn it off. He also offered Mama $100 to kill the parrot, and to get rid of the dog because they made way too much noise.

Later that afternoon he began knocking in the air with his right hand. He knocked and knocked again, and then dropped his hand and looked totally lost and confused. Wanting to help, I tried to think of what to say or do. The words, *Knock and it shall be opened to you, Seek and you shall find, Ask and it shall be given to you,* came to mind.

"Ask, Daddy, ask for what you want," I said. "They'll let you in."

He looked at me so angrily, and with such seriousness said, "And do what? Show them my driver's license?"

Not knowing what else to say, I said, "Daddy, they know you. They'll let you in."

Two years later I heard Dr. Bernie Siegel say that when you finally get to God someone asks you, "Who are you?" or "How do you want me to introduce you to God?"

If you give your name, or your profession, or actually anything that identifies you with something material or insignificant, they send you back with the admonishment, "Come back when you know who you are!"

I thought about my Daddy's response: "And do what? Show them my driver's license?" and believed Dr. Siegal's statement applied.

If I did it again I'd say, "Tell them you're home Daddy. Tell them your Father waits for you."

As the day wore on, things got even stranger.

That evening, Kristina decided not to come. She found it difficult seeing Daddy so weak. That left Mama, Debbie and me on guard for the night.

Daddy seemed to start to rest and let go. He got really peaceful, closed his eyes, and almost smiled. Then he opened his eyes, sneered, and looked really angry and scared at the same time. This happened in cycles, the peaceful stages lasting ten minutes at most. When I thought he saw unsettling images, I talked to him, telling him that he didn't have to see it, that Jesus and all the help he needed was there. Eventually he'd get peaceful again. He seemed frightened at times, and sometimes he made guttural noises that sounded like growling. Once when I tried to calm him down, he actually told me to "Get away you liar, you whore!" This reminded me of the movies, and my mom took this as a statement that Daddy did not want me around. I could not convince her that this did not come from Daddy. She couldn't explain the seeming personality differences, but called them spells.

Poor Debbie seemed about to go crazy. Not only did she not have the slightest understanding of my beliefs, she found what Daddy went through terribly disturbing. All of us did. Later, a severe round of anxiety seized Daddy. I knelt down and started praying. I didn't say the prayers we learned as children, but talking straight from my heart to any heavenly beings that might help my Daddy. I told Daddy to tell it to go away, that he needn't be afraid, that God waited for him.

My sister yelled at me. She told me I was crazy, made her crazy, made them all crazy. She wanted me to stop praying and acting like Daddy faced other beings. Strangely enough I wasn't afraid of whatever went on for me or for us, but I did worry about my father's agony. I wanted it to stop. I told Debbie I couldn't stop, that my Daddy was too important to me. She said she couldn't stand it anymore, that she'd leave, and she looked at Mama.

I can understand why she thought I had lost my mind. One minute I asked them to let Daddy do his own thing, not to talk to him and not try to bring him into our world, and the next minute there I plead with him. I really feel that divine intervention took place because I expected Mama to tell me to leave instead of letting Debbie leave. But instead she said, "Debbie, I don't want you to leave, but let's let Susan be with Daddy for a while." Debbie stormed out, slamming the door. Mama decided to get some rest and left me with Daddy for awhile.

Daddy calmed down for a while and started calling me "Shug" again. He then asked what upset me. I told him I felt bad for messing with him and everybody, but I also felt fear for him. Why would I risk having everyone hate me if it wasn't something I believed in? He smiled. I said, "Daddy I only know what I've seen, not what you've seen, but I've watched you do some incredible healing today. Am I right?" He said, "Yes. How do you know?"

I answered that the day had been pretty strange. I got quiet again and just sat with him. Then the personality shifts started again. I don't know why I thought I had anything to add to this situation, but I felt sure of it at the time. We were the only humans in the room. For some reason, I stood up and moved about four feet away from Daddy with my hands outstretched and prayed silently. I raised my arms, palms facing him. I normally don't do this nor had I heard of anyone else doing it. The room seemed to take on a golden glow, which I attributed to my exhaustion. Then, one of the times Daddy went back to his peaceful self, he looked at me in pure bliss. He said, "Wow, Shug, where did you get that gown?" His eyes looked so soft and open, that look that you only see when someone dies. The look goes to the depths of our souls when they can see through you, too. "Wow," he kept saying. "It's so beautiful." I told him I wore a T-shirt and shorts, and he said, "No, You are beautiful and your gown is just..." I then said, "I've probably had it forever," And he appeared to agree. He then closed his eyes again, and I told him how much I loved him. His face again began to change into that awful scowl. I don't know if something else inhabited his body or if this was a part of him, but I continued to pray. Not once during this whole conversation did I ever lower my hands. Suddenly I began to feel like I grew taller, wider, and would eventually pull apart. I could feel all of my individual cells, and at that moment the thought went through my head, not a voice, but a thought that I didn't recognize as mine.

A thought flashed through my mind: "If you get your father, you don't get your son."

It took me aback, and almost instantly I said to myself, "That's not true. Get away from me."

In reality, I don't get anybody. Who did I tell to get away from me? I hadn't thought of my son during these last few days, only my father. Why didn't this thought refer to my mother, my sister, my daughter, or my husband? Why not the others as when I was a young girl and feared for my Dad? And, why my son now?

I believe it's because I always thought of John as special, as my grandmother had promised. When I got pregnant with John, we'd already decided that our two girls were plenty. Because of my health, I wanted to avoid pregnancy and we took every precaution. Here he came anyway, my special son. He also came into a way of life that many would condemn, although that did not concern me. I felt concern because for two years he lost sight of the integrity and love inside him. The world and material things had tempted him to make many decisions that I worried about and that seemed to make his life more sordid and unhappy, alienating him from all those who loved him. More importantly, this whole incident made me aware of a dark, evil energy at work in this world that obviously had some investment in my Dad. I don't know why I have such a hard time saying "the devil", but it seems to give much more power to this evil than it deserves. With God in our hearts and minds nothing can sway us.

The more I felt like I was physically coming apart, the weaker I got. I even felt like I might die. I went to get Mom. She asked no questions. I went to bed and started sobbing uncontrollably. What if I had left him too soon? Who was I to think I could do anything? How presumptuous! Maybe if I could have just stayed a little longer he'd have understood. I called my husband, crying and said, "My father has given me such a gift. He has confirmed everything, everything I have believed. I've let him down and I owe him so much."

Poor Jim, what in the world did I expect him to think? That his wife had gone off the deep end? He tried to calm me down, to make me understand, and the more I said how much I owed my Daddy, the more it irritated him. He finally said, "Baby, didn't you say that your Daddy was giving you a gift?"

"Yes," I said.

My husband said, "Then you don't owe him anything, do you?"

"But I should have stayed with him. That being won't let go of him."

I suddenly saw colors floating up and away from me. I could see through these roses, blues, and violets in oval and circular shapes. They traveled right up from me and through the ceiling. I could not stop crying. I said, "Maybe, I'm going too, maybe I'm going too."

Jim said that wasn't true, and that I should just try to sleep. I told him I loved him, hung up and continued to cry and criticize myself for not staying longer, for not having enough courage to stay and help. As much as I believed that a person ultimately dies alone, I couldn't let go of the fact that Daddy needed me. Without me he'd be lost, perhaps not forever, but for the moment. I firmly believe that wherever our consciousness exists at the time of death, it will stay there until we decide to choose otherwise, but God will always welcome us home when we realize that we have a home to go to. If we don't choose God, He won't order us to do so. Daddy had already said he did not want to go to the light, that he didn't need any help. He didn't want to hear about heaven. He didn't think about love and happiness. He felt angry, unbelieving and, most of all, frightened; fear or love, nothing else exists.

I had a prescription for Xanax that I used only when I could not sleep. I decided to take one to calm me. I had given my sister several during the past few weeks, but I thought that I didn't need it. I wanted to stay in control of myself and remain as available and conscious as possible, but now I was falling apart. I finally started to doze when my husband and daughter arrived, startling me. At midnight, they walked into the bedroom to make sure I was all right. They had gotten in the car after my call and driven all the way from Austin to check on me.

Mom and Dad were quiet in the living room. When my sister left earlier in the evening in her understandable rage, she left the garage door open and the garage entrance to the house unlocked. This never happened in Daddy's house. If the Daddy of my youth had known of this, he'd have flown into a rage.

Mama had noticed them walking through the living room and just nodded. I took their arrival as a miracle. My angels had come. They asked if I needed to go home, but at this point I still thought Daddy needed me. They left, after hugging me and assuring me of their love and said I wasn't crazy, even if they thought differently. They stayed less than half an hour. They drove three hours to spend that precious time with me. I felt assured of their love. I instructed them to close and lock the doors. After all, I am my father's child.

I lay there fitfully saying the prayer of protection over and over, hoping for Daddy's forgiveness and Mama's understanding. I planned to call Bonnie, the hospice chaplain, in the morning for a reality check. I saw this strong Catholic woman as my rock. I didn't know another drama would unfold before I made that call.

At about 6 a.m. I awoke in a stupor. I had not slept for any real length of time. I thought I heard chanting, but I knew Mama better than to think she played that kind of music. I lay in the bed trying to make sense of it. Was I hallucinating? Was Daddy dead or breathing his last?

Suddenly I realized I could also hear Mama praying the Lord's Prayer and Hail Marys back to back, over and over. It sounded intense. I had never heard her pray like that, and never heard her so focused. I listened for a while and then my mind started to mess with me. Did Daddy want to hear this? I got up. When I reached the doorway into the living room I stood in awe. My Mom kneeled at my Daddy's right side next to the couch. She appeared as if in a trance, but still praying out loud. Daddy's right arm rested on her left shoulder. I stood and watched in admiration, and feeling the total beauty of this scene. Daddy looked peaceful. Mama prayed with all her heart. They were getting it!

Daddy opened his eyes and saw me across the room. He smiled and gestured for me to come join them. At least that's what I saw. As I got closer, silently he reached up to me and I took his hand, saying nothing. "All my prayers answered," I thought. The family I had always wanted at last, even if it came together at my Daddy's deathbed.

But my mother saw this as an intrusion on my part. She told me to let go of Daddy's hand. I did as she asked, although he did not let go of mine. She again yelled at me to let go. I told her I wasn't holding his hand, and then she bit me. When Mama went on to journal this event in her notes and wrote how angry she felt with me for interrupting, she says she thinks she pinched me. I had bite marks. I say this not to fault my mother, but to acknowledge another energy in the room, a darker, more demonic energy that did not want things to go harmoniously. She wrenched me away from Daddy, and I went back to my room again sobbing uncontrollably. I called several of my friends in Austin to see if someone could come and get me. They couldn't. I should have gone with Jim and Becca last night. I knew I could not drive myself. I called Bonnie and waited for a call back. I feared Mama would answer the phone, but as Divine Order had it, she didn't.

Bonnie seemed fascinated and also compassionate. She said, "I see, then you're definitely experiencing both the Light and the Darkness." She advised that I take a walk around the neighborhood and let off some energy. Scream or cry if I needed to, but get out of the house, clear my mind and then decide whether to go back to Austin or not. I went, I walked, I cried, I screamed, I prayed. I felt lost. Where had I gotten off thinking I could do anything for anyone? Everyone gets the help they need, and dying is a private, intimate thing. I went back, decided to take a shower and rest. Mama had called Debbie to come and help her.

In the shower I felt myself losing it again. I heard voices, breathing, screaming, etc. and had to talk myself out of it. This must be fatigue and an extraordinary experience, I knew. I also knew I didn't have time to lose it just yet. I tried to stay out of Mama's way, take care of myself, and help them if needed. If Mama needed me, she'd always ask. She truly did not understand that anyone else had feelings. When Michael, the nurse, arrived around noon, Daddy told him again that it was his heart that needed fixing.

Mama and Debbie told Michael I'd make lots of trouble and everyone felt tense. I felt I was dying too, and asked him to check my vital signs before he left.

They told him I behaved very strangely and prayed oddly. He came into the bedroom. He listened to my heart and took my blood pressure. My blood pressure was low, my heart rate rapid and my eyes dilated. He told me I needed rest. I asked if he felt the energies in the house. He replied that I obviously made everyone uncomfortable because of the strange things I talked about, and because of the way I had prayed the night before. I explained that I said only a prayer for the angels and Jesus to help my daddy stop seeing the thing that made him growl and grimace and feel angry.

I don't know now if I would do that sort of thing again, but I certainly had never gone through anything like that before. Also, I saw that Daddy did not like it. Michael said that he could feel a dark energy in the house, and that was the way it worked. Whenever everything started going smoothly, the energy put us at each other's throats. That certainly described the last six weeks. My stomach gurgled in a strange way for three days. I could feel it go straight up the center of my abdomen. Many times when I massage people they experience the same thing, and sometimes it seems like we communicate that way. This happened consistently with some clients. My stomach growled, then theirs, throughout the massage.

Of course, sometimes the bowel makes these noises during hunger or upset, but this always occurred during massage. In some kinds of bodywork, borborygmus or intestinal rumbling is accepted as a working sign of shifting energy. This always foreshadowed events for me. When I made my first communion in the first grade, my stomach got loud right before I went up to the altar. We were still fasting before and after communion then, and it always embarrassed me as a child, but my acupuncturist said, that maybe the rumbling represented communion to me. Anyway, Michael's stomach started making noise too. He said, "I don't know why that's happening. I just ate."

In my altered state I said, "I do. I think it's the Holy Spirit just letting me know that He is working in both of us."

Of course, that did it for Michael. He told me how when he preached on Sundays that when the Spirit came upon him he could preach for an hour, do the best sermon ever, and not remember any of it. He said this stomach noise certainly was not the Spirit. In his estimation, earthly bodily noises could not be spiritual. From then on, he felt I was not needed. I can't say that I blame him.

Chapter 8

The End of the Beginning

I got angry and told Mom of my plans to leave. I didn't know if I'd return, even for the funeral. I felt so hurt, and so sad. She didn't say anything then, but I don't really think she wanted me to leave. I decided to take another walk before driving myself home since I had not found a ride. I didn't want to disturb Jim again. When I got back I told Mama again that I was leaving, going home to get some rest, and if she needed me for anything, to call and I'd come as quickly as I could. I said I loved her, apologized, and said I obviously needed some rest. She agreed.

I sat with Daddy and told him how much I loved him, and that nothing could break our connection. I said I hoped he wasn't mad at me for all of the commotion I had caused. He didn't say much, but he did smile and say he loved me too. I didn't think he'd die before I came back this time. I can't remember how I drove home. Surely God must have sent extra angels to help me. Everything looked blurry, but not because of tears. I felt numb. I wanted to get home to my husband and family. I wanted my bed, and comfort. When I did get home and told my daughter the story, she said, "Which of you opened all of these doors to the other side, you or your dad? You'd better take care when you don't know what exists out there." I replied that I wasn't sure, but that I wasn't afraid of anything except Daddy losing his way.

When we went to bed that night, I felt fragile, weak and spacy. Imagine that. As I sat on the edge of the bed before lying down I felt a thousand little fingers poking me in the back. I sat, breathed and tried to figure out what I really felt. The sensation almost felt like when I stood back in the living room with Daddy. Now not only was I coming apart, but something bumped up against me and made me feel like I might just explode. I turned to my husband and said, "Are you trying to send me good energy or vibes or something?"

He said, "No, I'm just looking at you."

"Well, stop it!" I demanded, and started to cry.

He held me for a long time and I finally went to sleep.

When I woke up the next morning I felt like death warmed over. Jim went to work. Becca left, too. I called Bonnie in San Antonio to let her know I got home safely and then fell back asleep. I woke up again and tried to go into the living room, but could hardly drag myself around. I got to the sofa and decided to call on my resources, folks of the same mind, folks who could do some bodywork to help me reconnect with the world.

Oddly enough, I found none of the folks I called home and left messages for Ward, the acupuncturist, Poppy, the "hands on" person, and Taki, the massage therapist. I needed to feel my body and be nurtured and loved. I thought at first that I felt okay.

However, every time I made a call I said, "This is Susan. I know I'm calling last minute but I have to ask. I've been in San Antonio with my Daddy, he's dying, and ...." then I'd start to cry and finishing the sentence took effort. "I need help."

Even then I knew how much like my father I was. We asked for help with difficulty. I believe God ran this whole show because Ward called back almost immediately and told me he could see me in 45 minutes. I'd had to wait two weeks to see him before. Poppy called back, too, saying she had a full load that day, but suggested the next day. I scheduled the appointment and thanked her. Taki called too, and made an appointment for Friday. When I got to Ward's I could not stop rattling. He placed the needles as I told him my story. He said he thought I was too attached and needed to get grounded, that I invested too much of myself in this and that I needed to leave it alone. I needed energy. I couldn't understand why everyone did not share my awe of this experience. He gave me an herbal roll-up or fruit bar to help ground me, told me to drink plenty of water and rest. He hugged me and I went home and fell into a deep sleep.

Before falling asleep I prayed for Daddy to hear me, and asked forgiveness if I made dying harder for him. I apologized for the altercations that Mama, Debbie and I acted out in front of him. I said, "Please, Daddy, please forgive me, please remember that I only wanted to help you die easily, please remember how much I love you." Although I slept deeply, I remember a vivid dream from that day. Elephants followed me everywhere. I was on an island and went from house to house, and these elephants stuck their heads or trunks inside. If I went outside they'd follow right behind me or walk next to me, uncomfortably close. As I began to wake up I asked, "What does this dream mean?" Almost instantly the thought came to me, "An elephant never forgets!" I started laughing and crying at the same time. Daddy had always taken me to the zoo, he had always prided himself on educating us about animals and I believed that he sent me this message in a dream. He knew what I tried to do for him, and he'd remember.

I got up about three. Poppy called to say that she wanted to work on me that evening about 6:15. I said wait until tomorrow. I knew she must be tired, and I knew she'd find me a mess to work on. She assured me that she wanted to work that evening although she didn't know where the energy came from. I still had a hard time getting from one room to another.

Around 4:30 I started feeling better. I even ventured into the living room and told my honey that I might eat something later. Shortly before 5:30 my Mom called. "Sue," she said, "Daddy's gone. It was beautiful, and I have stories to tell you." I said, "Wonderful." Earlier, I'd have felt upset that she hadn't called me earlier, that I hadn't been there. The first time I drove home when Daddy stayed in the hospital, I felt like a nervous wreck all the way to Austin and back thinking that he might die without me. But for some reason, now I felt totally content, joyful at Mama's description of the death as beautiful, pleased that she said she would tell me stories. With me there, she'd feel differently. Now Mama had seen and experienced this glory with no analysis from me. I felt a connection to Daddy, and all appeared right with the world.

They set the funeral for Saturday, and Mama said I didn't need to come down right away. She felt okay and Debbie and Kristina were there to help. She said the casket would be closed and that seemed fine to me. I didn't need to see his body. We were connected.

I called his sister, Barbara Jean, to tell her the news. Even though she had seen him the weekend before, she couldn't believe that he'd died. Then she got really upset when I told her that Mom set the funeral for Saturday. How could she? It fell on Easter weekend, and what about flowers? We couldn't reach all of the people who'd want to come. What was wrong with everyone, and, finally, why close the casket?

By Friday afternoon Mama decided to leave the casket open and have visitation on Friday evening. I opted not to go to San Antonio until Saturday. I had plenty of things to do in Austin. I called to tell Barbara Jean about visitation and she also opted not to go. We offered her a ride to the funeral on Saturday, as did my daughter Lysa, and she declined. She was in shock and too angry.

Chapter 9

Signs and Wonders

I'm getting ahead of myself now. Only an hour ago I barely felt able to get around the apartment. I just started to feel more like myself again, and I felt relief that Daddy finally reached some peace. Pleased to get an appointment with my friend Poppy, I drove myself the few blocks to her house arriving as close to 6:15 as I could. As I stretched out on the table Poppy said, "Susan, you weren't supposed to go with your Daddy, you know?" I wondered why she said that. It seemed strange that other people could tell I wasn't all here, or out of my body, because to me I seemed quite myself. A little tired, a little frazzled, but shouldn't I be? I hadn't slept except for six hours, uninterrupted, until that day.

The same day my Daddy actually died, Poppy worked on me for the whole hour, and mentioned I could use a lot more. I made an appointment for the next week or so, but as I got down off the table and she checked me out I said with great conviction, "I'm back!" It felt like a ton of burdens rose off me. Yet I felt more solid than I had in weeks. I couldn't believe how free I felt, how full of joy. Then almost immediately I started to wonder why I wasn't crying, or feeling a great loss. I fully believed then, and to this day, that my Daddy and I needed to accomplish something together, and we did it. I'm not sure exactly what, but I feel his presence every day in more ways than ever. I miss only one part of him, the same part I missed during his life. I feel so connected to him now.

I felt good enough to stay up for the 10 o'clock news, and heard about an earthquake that had occurred around 7:30 p.m. that evening. We did not feel it at the apartment, but people all over Austin did. My friends downtown felt it as they sat on their balcony. Glenn and his mother were visiting and taking care of his partner, also near death. However, Jerry didn't fight or deny it. I said to Jim that the earthquake was Daddy breaking through, that maybe he was the 100th monkey after all. I joked about it, but in my heart I meant it. If my hardheaded father made it to God, and God waited on him to get ready as he waited on the one lost sheep or the prodigal son, that meant all of us had worth. God waits for us with his arms open.

Friday morning I arranged for flowers from my family. I sent them to my Mom and Dad, thanking them for everything. I wanted a haircut but nobody had an opening. I went for a massage and discovered that my body hurt all over. I went to visit with Glenn, to check on Jenny's progress. I wanted to let Jerry know that Daddy died and that life went on. I talked with my sister, Debbie, who told me one of Daddy's last statements: "Lord, come get me in a hurry, pick me up so I can go!" In my Mom's notes, she says she had a hard time deciphering what he said at the end because he was so weak and speaking so softly you could hardly hear him. She couldn't tell if he said "Laura" or "Lord" but felt pretty sure he said Lord. He grabbed her and told her to kiss him. She said he kissed her like he hadn't kissed her in a long time, then said "Lord, Lord, hurry, hurry get me up!" That made me cry, but again, not in sadness but joy. Daddy made it. I knew he had, and I, in my mind, had proof.

The headlines told all about the earthquake, and the line that caught my eye pinpointed the center in West Texas, in Alpine. And then the statement, "It was felt as far away as San Antonio at the Air Control Tower, and on the ground in Austin." The earthquake destroyed little and harmed no one. Again, in the paper September 13, 1997, in the LM Boyd trivia column, I saw the question, "Which of the United States is least likely to get an earthquake?" The answer: Either Texas or Florida. Both claim the bottom of the quake likelihood list.

Now I know people can say I'm reaching, but my Daddy found release and made his way through the spheres, in my belief. Though I remained here on earth in Austin, Daddy had broken free in San Antonio. I took the quake as a sign Daddy made the right choice. The next week, when I told my acupuncturist my thoughts on the matter, he looked at me incredulously and said, "Susan, you actually think the world needed to know when your father died?" And it wasn't until that moment that I realized that the earthquake got national and international attention, but I saw it only as a sign to me.

Saturday morning my children, Jim and I all left for the funeral at 9:30 a.m. People filled the small chapel. My father's friends came, as well as my aunts and uncles and one of his cousins. The casket stayed open, and as much as I protested seeing bodies all of my life, I did look at Daddy's. He did not look like the Daddy I had known, but he did look peaceful and content. I saw that smile of contentment only during the last few days of his life, and I'm glad the funeral home captured it.

My granddaughter rushed into the chapel and exclaimed, "Pawpaw's not in heaven, he's right here!" which gave all of us a little relief from the obvious tension and grief. My Mom held together rather well, as did Debbie. I still didn't cry. In fact, I felt almost euphoric. I'm sure a lot of people did not understand. More than one person expressed concern. They'd say, "Susan, you don't have to be so strong," or "Susan, it's okay to cry," or "Are you and your Mom okay?"

I reassured them that Daddy had given me

everything I ever wanted and more in his last weeks. If he still walked this earth, we'd probably be at odds, but now he'd left the bonds of his pain. I feel sure he had loved me enough to experience all that I believed, out loud.

The minister, Father Jack, gave a beautiful eulogy, much better than most of the "church" funerals I attended in the last few years. He talked about how loving my father had been, how everybody loved him, how he had played with us all the time as children, and of his love for animals. He read a very moving poem about death, that likened dying to "just being in the next room." I felt relief and release.

As we got into the limo for the trip to the cemetery I asked Mom where Father Jack had gotten his information on Daddy. She told me she had given him a copy of the book she had written about our family entitled *Poor Li'l Alice*.

I really didn't like the book, and as far as I knew her description of her sisters, my sisters and Daddy did not fit any of the people that I knew. She had it printed about four years prior to Daddy's illness and no one felt thrilled with it. In the book, she said Daddy had a German temper and described him as just plain mean. How did Father Jack write such a beautiful eulogy from Mama's book? Maybe he just ad libbed.

My sister Kristina suffered the most at the funeral. She just couldn't leave Daddy's side, and really did not want them to close the casket. She had put her graduation picture in with him. She didn't want him to forget her. My husband Jim and my ex-husband Charlie served as pallbearers. My daddy loved Charlie. Actually I always felt my parents liked him more than me. At least they understood him. Charlie closed himself off emotionally and didn't make waves. I, on the other hand, always explored the meaning of things, letting everyone know exactly how I felt and why. I always wanted my family to acknowledge that I did exist. None of them thought that necessary.

After the cemetery we went to my Mom's and visited. Everyone opened and closed the refrigerator, getting drinks. Children ran everywhere. I went to the refrigerator to get soda and as I opened it an entire shelf literally jumped off the door onto the floor. This embarrassed me, and as I cleaned up, Kristina said from across the room, "Well, Susan, didn't you just say the other day that Daddy liked to embarrass you?" I had to say yes, but hoped a faulty shelf caused this. After another 30 to 45 minutes of others going in and out of the refrigerator, it happened again with me. I do believe that personalities continue after death, so maybe Dad teased me now as he did all my life. I stayed away from the refrigerator the rest of the day.

As several of us stood in the kitchen talking, I also realized that my favorite cousin wore a tie with hundreds of monkeys on it, a strange tie for a funeral. The hundredth monkey?

When we got home I went searching for *Poor L'il*

Alice. I don't think I even took time to get undressed, and I know I didn't sit down but searched until I found it. I opened it immediately to the passages on Daddy and began to cry. It was beautiful, like someone rewrote the whole thing. Father Jack had taken everything he said directly from the book, and even more importantly, I found another message to me.

The second paragraph started, "My father used to say Walt had a photographic mind. This is true because he remembers like an elephant."

I immediately went back to my dream of Thursday afternoon, with the elephants chasing me, and my conviction that my father sent me a message. The next morning I talked with Aunt Jo because she, too, voiced concern about the relationship between my Mom and me. I said I was great and in love with Mom, and I know she thought I had gone over the edge. I told her the story of Father Jack's rendition of my father's life as told by Mom and she said, "You do know what she wrote about me, don't you?" I did. And when I read it years ago, I, too, thought it extremely rude. I got the book, and reread it to her.

She couldn't believe it. The difference was reading it with love, seeing it with love. The inflections related nothing but love. What made it so negative before? Did we all come from a different place? What about Mama? As I go over it now, I see only beautiful pages. I see Mama's weakness and strength, and the naiveté that she demonstrates now appears more like childlike innocence rather than the selfish woman I thought I'd endured all of my adult years. Then I was wrong, but that doesn't change the feelings and hurts I experienced.

Easter Sunday, April 16, 1995, Jerry Shaw, my friend, passed away about 8 a.m. Glenn called right away and I went to see him and Jerry's mom. What perfect timing. Jerry, I felt sure, orchestrated all of this not only so I could support Glenn, but Easter morning just seemed like Jerry. He died so much more peacefully than my Dad.

He knew what was happening and accepted it, embraced it. Jerry's mom told Glenn that two or three days before he died, he opened his eyes out of a seeming deep sleep and said, "The Light! Jesus!" and just as quietly closed his eyes and went back to sleep. We can learn much about the experience of nearing death, if only we will take the time to watch, listen and accept.

Back at home, I sat down to read the paper, only to see more reports on the earthquake. This time I read that the thirteenth aftershock had occurred at 9:33 a.m. Saturday morning. Strange, they had closed the casket at approximately that time. In some cultures the number 13 signifies the end or death.

Weeks went by and I could not shut up. I told anyone I thought might listen what I had to say. I talked to family, clients, authors of spiritual books that I met when my husband and I worked at Guadalupe

River Ranch. I wrote thank-you notes to all the hospice workers for their support and help, and then called everyone I had known in the last eight years who helped me get to the place where I could love and help my family through this. No one seemed as excited by my story as me. If they thought Daddy hallucinated, they were sure I did, too, particularly when I told them of the night that I heard, "If you get your father, you don't get your son." But I knew it was real. Two beings battled for my father's soul.

A week or so later another article about the earthquake appeared. Billy Porterfield, a contributing writer for the *Statesman*, printed a map showing the epicenter of the quake at Cathedral Mountain, between Diablo Platform and Delaware Basin. Symbolically, Cathedral and Diablo made perfect sense. The Cathedral represented God, or spirituality. The fight occurred between Diablo, the devil, and Delaware. But what did Delaware represent? In May, 1997, I finally decided to look it up.

The encyclopedia quotes Thomas Jefferson saying, "Delaware is a jewel among the states." A poet once wrote that "Delaware is like a diamond, diminutive, but having inherent value." and "Delaware is smaller than any state except Rhode Island, but its importance is much greater than its size."

So was Delaware the event or a person? There was a struggle, no one can deny that. Plus the owner of the piece of property that Cathedral Mountain sits on was named Walter. This can't be just coincidence. Consciousness is changing. Later I found in Mama's notes that at one point Daddy said something about Delaware losing the Democrats. This statement had absolutely nothing to do with anything at the time, but she wrote it down as some of the nonsense he said. And right after that he said, "Educate to the best of your ability, that's all you can do." Did he mean that for me?

The passage of time convinces me more about exactly what did happen, at least on one level. These are the things I know versus what I don't know, which is plenty. I do believe in reincarnation. I do believe that we either choose or are designated to a certain family, and groups of people to learn from and to help us remember our identity in relationship to God. We have free will, although not enough of us realize that we create what happens in our lives. Not God or the devil, but us. God exists inside each of us, loving us enough to let us do our own thing, and being a real, personal friend when we desire it. The devil, or our own minds, constantly try to convince us of our separateness, that we can do it all by ourselves, without acknowledging God. In a meditation retreat I attended in 1998, when I asked God just what He wanted from us, I heard a resounding "Acknowledge my Reality." That's all. With reincarnation we reap as we have sown, and the more separate we make ourselves in the previous life, the harder our lives will be the next time. We always have the means to change it all. God's grace suffices for all things, but as long as we deny our part in this play, we wallow in victimhood. We think we live at our parents' mercy, or our colleagues', or the environment, or God's, or the devil's. We refuse to acknowledge we have a choice. I believe God wants us as companions, and Edgar Cayce said that only man got the choice to deny his God. God gave us the capacity, not to fall down in adoration, even though His Power and Might deserve it, but to possess as much power and grace as He has. He said that.

We ate the fruit of the knowledge of good and evil. We decided that we knew right and wrong, good and bad. We started judging, not accepting that the Universal Laws of Nature are positive and negative and continually changing.

God obviously didn't consider nakedness evil. Didn't He ask Adam, "Who told you you were naked?" He talked and visited with Adam and Eve daily until they ate of the tree of the knowledge of good and evil and their minds convinced them they were separate, and not a part of God. He still searched them out and spoke to them, even to their children. We remain a part of God, made in His image and likeness. We just have to remember it. And my God is real! Flesh and blood real! Look around you So is yours! They are the same *one.*

On January 25, 1996, I received another

confirmation of my belief that everything we experience comes from consciousness expressing itself, whether we realize it or not. While giving a massage to one of my clients I asked if her partner planned on getting a tattoo. She said Sylvia was trying temporary tattoos to see what she really wanted. I remarked that Daddy had a tattoo, a butterfly on his forearm that I had dearly loved. It fascinated me from toddlerhood.

I can't remember what he said about it years ago, but I believe he'd speak more favorably then. Pat, my client, said a butterfly is sort of a strange tattoo for a man, especially a World War II veteran. Her dad had a skull and crossbones with a snake and sailor cap. The more benign ones of that era featured hearts with "Mom" on them, or naked ladies.

Then I recalled that prior to my Dad's last trip to the hospital he fell in the kitchen. His skin had thinned so from the medications he took, that it sometimes broke at the slightest touch. He fell on the arm with the butterfly, and the tattoo broke. I think that reminded him the time had arrived for his true spirit to emerge. I also believe this same spirit chose the butterfly 50 years before, because for the last few years his bitter self hated it and quite often said that getting the tattoo turned out to be one of the most stupid things he had ever done in his life. When it tore in the fall, my mom reaffirmed that "finally we can get rid of that thing." To me, metamorphosis!

Did you know that children in the concentration camps during the holocaust drew butterflies on themselves and the walls? Butterflies symbolize transition. When an automobile accident killed my children's father in 1999, a butterfly T-shirt he bought for his wife remained unstained. It was a sign to us all.

Chapter 10

Dreams and Things

So, what happened after all the phenomena? We all dreamed things. My sister Debbie dreamed that she, Mama and I fell asleep in the same room, and that she woke up and Daddy sat next to me, just looking at me and smiling. She tried to wake Mama and me but couldn't. Daddy didn't say anything, but it seemed real to her.

Another time, she dreamed about Daddy as he appeared most of our lives. In this dream, Kristi told him something, and then Daddy grabbed her and started yelling at her. Debbie intervened. When she woke up the next day she realized how she'd romanticized Daddy since his death. She didn't cry for a while. In another dream she visited my grandmother's and saw Mama and Daddy walking across the front yard to the birdbath. In the dream, she started to cry. Daddy told her not to cry because Mama cried all day. She said he looked thin and older, but well and healthy.

My little sister Kristina had a dream right after Daddy died in which he got really upset because Mama got so active. Within a couple of weeks of his death, she returned to her usual walks in the morning with friends. She volunteered at the hospital, joined a grief group, took line-dancing lessons, and went on short trips with women from the groups she joined. The Daddy we knew would not like this. If personalities continue, this dream made sense. Daddy had lessons to learn on the other side. Catholics have purgatory, the Tibetans have the Bardols, and I'm not sure what else, but I believe we continue to heal.

The following year, on Father's Day, Kristi dreamed about him on the way home from a work trip. In real life, Kristi just found out she was pregnant. In her dream she went out to eat with him, and she said it seemed very real. She awoke, saddened by his absence.

Mama dreamed about walking with Daddy. She knew he was dead, but they had a comfortable and loving conversation. The dream comforted her.

My sister Debbie told me about two more noteworthy dreams. I did not remember any of mine, if I had any, for about six months. I wondered why he didn't comfort me. During this time I said I didn't need any comfort. So one night as I went to sleep I prayed, "Daddy please let me see you. If what I believe happened truly did, and you're there, please let me feel you. I know you don't need me hanging on, but I want a dream, too." Some time that night I dreamed. My husband and I sat in the living room of our apartment. On the chair next to the window sat the Chihuahua that Daddy gave me at age eight. I petted "Tinker" and told Jim all about him. I told Jim the dog's registered name: "Senor El Cobre." As I petted him, his hair fell out in tufts. My husband asked how old he was, and I replied, "Daddy gave him to me when I was about eight, so that makes him about 41 years old."

Even in the dream I realized that comment was absurd, and I woke up almost in tears. I felt upset to be dreaming about a dog when I wanted to dream about Daddy. Then I heard, again not a voice, but more like a thought or telepathy, Daddy laughing and saying, "I knew you would figure it out Shug. You were always so smart." Then I had to laugh.

Still, this did not truly satisfy me. I wanted to see Daddy, not Tinker. We're never happy with what we get, even when it's much more than what we asked for. If it had been Daddy in the dream, I could say it was just my mind, but the dog came out of nowhere.

Sometime later when I remembered and doubted the "hands-on" events and Daddy's seeming release after each episode, I dreamed I stood beside a big, tall bed. Daddy sat in the bed and I leaned on it with my elbows, asking questions. Then I explained to him what I thought had happened. I said that I didn't want to make stuff up from my point of view, so could he please tell me what had happened? He said, "That sounds about right," and laughed. We then said good-bye and I knew that I wouldn't see him again for a long while. I felt profound love and I woke up in tears.

In another dream, I am my age now, talking to a young Daddy as we sat at a sidewalk cafe in Paris. We were very romantic. We didn't kiss or even touch, but I felt an incredible amount of love. I don't know what that means.

Barbara Jean, Daddy's sister, dreamed that Daddy, Mommie and Pop came to see her. They all looked fine and happy. They told her she couldn't come yet because she wasn't dressed well enough. Her shoes were not quite right, either. She felt relieved about that since she didn't want to go anyway. I still wonder if the reference to shoes symbolized the soul (sole).

Other "Daddy sightings": Before I started dreaming about Daddy, I got hypnotized. A psychologist practiced in hypnosis hypnotized me in trade for a massage. Daddy was alive in this episode, about sixty years old, and very fit and handsome. He came out of a big building that looked like a library or school, with lots of steps and pillars. You could see through the building, like glass. He came down the stairs and told me, "It's all true, Shug. You don't have to worry. It's all true." To the left I saw several friends that had died two years before Daddy. I realized that Daddy was the greatest teacher of all. While he wasn't always the Daddy that I wanted when he lived, I needed him in order to realize my full potential. How much he must have loved our family. I started to cry. When I came back to full consciousness the hypnotist said, "Susan, I'm supposed to tell you it's true." I did not talk during my experience.

Becca, my daughter, had a waking encounter with Daddy. In her early twenties she belonged to a charismatic church. Born again, she worked at the church almost every day and sang and felt blessed. Then after some hard life lessons she came to live with us again in 1991. She stopped going to church. Shortly after Daddy died, she came home from work one Wednesday, took her usual nap, got up and announced that she was going to church. I thought she went to see an old boyfriend, but when she got back I realized she'd gone to church. She smiled from ear to ear, and said, "Your Daddy's doing great! I saw him during praise and he was laughing his butt off. I have never seen him so happy. I guess that's why I had to go to church tonight." She hasn't gone back since. I asked her if she saw Daddy with her eyes open or closed. She said she didn't remember, but that light surrounded him.

After a really transformational week in October, 1996, I ran errands feeling like all was right with the world. As I opened the car door to go into a massage school, a song came on the radio by Celine Dion. I had not heard it before, at least consciously. Titled

"Because You Loved Me", its words touched me to the core and the tears streamed down my face.

Certain phrases had a particularly poignant meaning for me. I heard her sing, "I'd lost my faith, you gave it back to me," and then, "You gave me faith, because you believed." I could not help but think of Daddy. "You were my strength when I was weak. I'm everything I am because you loved me."

As it turns out, Celine Dion wrote it for her father, but this had to be a message from Daddy.

This happened over a year after his death, and it seemed so real. Almost immediately the old skeptic in me came back. "Susan, who do you think you are? What about your mother's love for your Daddy? Why do you think you're so special? Why would your Daddy or God speak to you over the radio?"

I chalked it up to my overactive imagination. Maybe I hadn't grieved for Daddy and just missed him. When I got back into the car ten minutes later, I don't know if I changed the station or not. But I heard the song again. I started laughing and thanking God, and then almost immediately tried to dismiss it, just like my hardheaded Daddy would have done. I drove to a bookstore about three or four blocks away to pick up a book to give away, Final Gifts. I found the book, paid for it, got back in the car, turned the ignition on and heard the song again. I stopped doubting that this held a message for me, until December 1997.

I'd suffered that day. I felt depressed after closing

my massage office. I had not completed this book. I sank deeper into debt, and thought maybe I was crazy after all. As I drove home from the bank the song came on and I said out loud, "Oh, Daddy, I so much needed to hear that!"

Again, my mind started to argue, asking me if the song played only when I needed to hear it. Immediately, without commercial break, the next song that played was "Step by step, every move you make, every breath you take, I'll be watching you." I breathed a sigh of relief. Years have passed and as I sit down to play the song at home, I've made it my song to my dad instead of his to me: "Because you loved me."

At about the same time as the first radio episode, my sister Kristina had gone to Mama's to pick up my Daddy's college graduation ring, and, as she started talking to Mom about the ring, the song "The Wind Beneath My Wings" came on. She and Daddy both held this song as special, and she said that neither she nor Mama had heard it playing on the radio before. If we stay aware, watch, and listen, we can recognize signals all around us.

Kristina turned 30 in May 1997. I gave her a card with chimpanzees on the front. As she opened it, a cross hanging on the wall behind me jumped right off and landed two or three feet away. It didn't slide or bounce, it jumped. Just like the refrigerator shelves jumped off the day of the funeral. Our eyes got as big as half dollars, and then we started laughing. Our loved ones stay with us after death, yet some people still trivialize these events, refusing to see the reality.

Chapter 11

I Know the Future, God Wins

The words, "If you get your father, you don't get your son!" returned to haunt me on Memorial Day Weekend, 1995, one month after Daddy's death. My in-laws came to visit and we made a family party.

On Sunday evening my daughter and her husband and four children came over. Becca also came, and my son did, too. I didn't get to see him very often at that time because he managed a nightclub in town that stayed open after hours every weekend. I visited this club several times when it first opened, but it changed. While successful, the atmosphere changed. I remember warning John that he needed to get away from it now and then because nobody could remain healthy living in that kind of atmosphere all the time. But he worked hard, sometimes staying up more than forty-eight hours at a time to keep tabs on it all.

His visit that evening surprised me. He looked so handsome. He got down on the floor with the grandkids and played. My in-laws were amazed at how he had grown, his appearance and his success. I had not told them of his job, and they didn't know he was gay. They were extremely anti-homosexual, and the older I get the more I believe that sometimes not telling makes the most sense. We had a wonderful evening and it pleased me to see everyone together. The next morning as we sat around the breakfast table reminiscing about the night before the phone rang. The caller, a friend of John's, cried and talked almost incoherently about John. "It's horrible, Mama G, it's horrible. It's John. He's in jail. He had a gun."

I shook and cried. What could have happened in eight hours to change everything?

John locked himself in his office with a gun. He must have considered suicide. The staff and his friends kept trying to get him to respond and finally called the police. He fired the gun, not at anyone but just to get them to leave him alone, not realizing that the police had arrived. When he learned this, he put down the gun and opened the door, and they arrested him. They kept him on suicide watch for a few days in the county jail, and released him on bail a week later.

Loving, sensitive and honest, John graduated in the top ten of his class. What drove him to this? And, what now? Had I lost him? I knew in my heart that only the grace of God saved him that night. I thought it miraculous that John hurt no one and the police did not kill him. I also knew that I couldn't reach him. He loved us, but felt humiliated and embarrassed. How could he live with himself now?

All of this was his choice, to think he could do it alone without being connected to anyone. At the same time I knew that God worked through John's higher self to show him the rewards of the life he led. This was his turning point, but it frightened all of us.

My daughter and I both knew, though, that God gave us an answer to our prayers. She even said this the morning we got the call, "Mom, our prayers are answered. He's out of that bar."

It took months, but John turned into a blessing to all those he touches. He lives only a couple of blocks from me and I see him now more than ever.

Now what did the other side have to do with all of this? If he had committed suicide would it have won? Who is "it"? Does the devil exist? Is it just energy? Is there really a battle? Someone or some thing spared me the punishment of my own foolishness with suicide attempts. I tried not once but several times both before and after my divorce, and once, in 1980, my heart stopped only to come back in the emergency room. After that incident I've never entertained the thought of suicide again. I transformed my life, but not overnight. I did it step by step. I figured, quite regretfully I might add, that even God did not want me at that point, and that He must have something else in mind. What a surprise.

Back to John—Early that Monday morning a

storm hit the city. A loud clap of thunder woke me up, and I said out loud, “John”, not knowing why. I felt the same way I had during the storms the week Daddy died. As I began this passage, actually as I typed the words “If you get your Dad, you don’t get your son”, I heard an unusually loud clap of thunder on a sunny day. It ushered in a long awaited cold front.

Why don’t I feel afraid anymore? I believe it’s because I know in my heart, and now in my mind that like a bumper sticker I saw the other day, “I know the future—God wins”. And, how could He not? He made it all. In the book of Isaiah it says, “There is only one God, he made the Light and the Dark, good and evil both he made.” And then in the book of John, Jesus reminds us, “Did you not know that ye are gods?” We decide which way we want to go. We just need to keep our minds set on Him and we don’t walk alone.

I also know now that everything is the expression of consciousness, but you must be conscious to start seeing it. Observe the people you know who have suffered a loss. Or watch yourself. Bereaved partners or spouses almost inevitably start remodeling, or move, or start building a new physical dwelling after they go through the cleaning out stage. It seems to express the actual letting go of the old and the start of a new way of life. Those who remain in the same surroundings and don’t get rid of things usually end up stuck and grieve a lot longer. Many quickly join their spouse on the other side. I don’t mean that you must purge and rebuild, or that you must do it in a certain amount of time. Just watch and notice the dynamics.

Even I came home from Daddy's funeral and cleaned closets and drawers on that very day. Again, I believe that even weather is an expression of consciousness, collective consciousness. All of us, not just individually, but ever so often when needed, someone of definite strength, either positive or negative, leaves a sign to the world.

If everything is energy, positive and negative, then isn't it just possible that we project those battles into the spheres, such as earthquakes, for instance? In fact, I read that quakes and storms occurred when Jesus died, and when Buddha was born. The *Tibetan Book of Living and Dying* says that earthquakes occur when an enlightened person consciously dies.

Chapter 12

Healing On A Grand Scale

In June I tried to get Mom and my sisters to go to the coast for a weekend. I still had some connections that enabled me to get an excellent rate at a beautiful condo in Port Aransas. Debbie and Kristina and Mama all agreed to go. I made the reservations. The weekend arrived and both of my sisters changed their plans. Nevertheless, I committed myself. I wanted to go to the coast, and I knew Mama had always loved going with Daddy, so off we went. We had such a good time. Although Mama and I don't agree on very much, some way or another we took care of each other, and had a really good time. I didn't feel so much like a daughter, but more like her peer. As much as my sisters' backing out disappointed me, I feel sure it changed the dynamic for Mama and me. Our fun would have decreased.

I found sand dollars on the beach. I never found them before or since, but that trip I found a bucketfull.

We spent three days and two nights without an argument, although by the time we got home my nerves felt raw, and I'm sure hers did, too. Our relationship continues to grow and a mutual appreciation keeps expanding. She's a wonderful person. That does not mean our trials have ended, as you will see.

Changes occurred rapidly. A friend of my Dad's from his childhood, Ed, started calling and stopping by to check on Mama. His wife had passed away only a year or two earlier. They went for rides and ate at the restaurants they liked. Ed told Mom that Daddy had asked him to take care of her. Before experiencing the dying process, Daddy had always had a jealous streak.

During the summer, Mama started talking about someone she had met at the church grief group. His wife had passed away in February, and Daddy in April. We could tell that something went on between them, but we couldn't really believe that she felt serious about someone so soon after Daddy's death. But we heard a different tone to her voice. She asked my husband and me if we wanted to come down the weekend before my birthday for dinner at the Old San Francisco Steakhouse, a place for family celebrations. I already had plans, but we agreed to go as I didn't want to seem ungrateful and I did want to see everybody. But as the time approached I decided to go with my original plans. I thought going there would be too hard on everyone because Daddy had always been with us before. When I called to tell Mom she said okay, but that she had to cancel with everyone (meaning Tom, her new friend), after she had already made arrangements. When I found out that she had planned to bring Tom I felt relief that I had stayed true to myself. If I had gone to that birthday celebration and met him unannounced, I feel sure I'd have made a scene. Again, I know Mama did not mean to be hurtful, but she just did not take our feelings into account. The next week I went down to have lunch with her. When I got to the house I got to meet Tom, again a surprise. I could see Mama's nervousness at introducing him. She repeated that Tom was her friend, they had so much in common, and he'd helped her so much. I'd never seen Mama like this. She acted like a teenager. She giggled and blushed and made fun of him. My like for Tom surprised me. He seemed so loving, down to earth and real. He was easygoing and laughed. He didn't get upset even when we changed our choice of restaurant several times before making a decision, and he really seemed to care about Mom.

One thing led to another. Tom came to our first Thanksgiving without Daddy, and to the Christmas celebration also. I don't think Mama had time to really grieve Daddy's death, but maybe she grieved all during his illness. Or maybe she didn't need to grieve, and Tom and Mom were gifts to each other from God. Neither of them had to go through the holidays alone, without their partners. Both sets of children wanted them to have their happiness. That does not mean we accepted it all calmly But I didn't like Mama seemingly ignoring us and paying so much attention to his children. After all, Daddy died, not all of us.

In February 1996, Mama and Tom decided to get married. This caused a little confusion, because although we all approved we'd hoped they would wait a whole year after Daddy's death. Why a year? I don't know, but it just seemed the thing to do. That hurt Mama's feelings. She wanted a life of her own. "After all you have your men, and your children. Shouldn't I have the same?" she asked us. It's all perspective. My sisters and I just wanted to feel included.

They married June 8, 1996, and have enjoyed their honeymoon ever since. They have traveled: cruises, European vacations, California, etc. Mama thought these things frivolous before. Most of all, she enjoyed herself. She loves dancing, and Tom dances with her whenever she wants, at home or out. God does work in mysterious ways, and I fully believe God rewarded her with Tom for staying true to her convictions and to Daddy throughout their lives together. I don't know that much about Tom's life with his wife and eight children, but from what I have gathered they loved each other from a young age. They'd lived life to the fullest and expressed their love always. I truly believe Tom sees Mama as a gift that allows him to continue enjoying his life as a reward for devotion to his family life before. It all seems perfect to me.

For the first time in her life, my sister Debbie studies the Bible actively as a member of the BSF, a national group. Both of us went to Catholic school as young girls. I bought everything, and she bought none of it. Now God makes up a conscious part of her life, and I again credit Daddy's death experience for this awakening. She did not seek this, but her employers live as Christians. They supported and comforted Debbie during our family crisis. Through their dealings with trauma and tragedy in their own families, drawing on their faith and each other demonstrated to her the blessings of that faith. It is by our example that we give testimony to God.

My youngest sister remarried and now has three beautiful children. Her husband, Victor, lost his mother not long before Daddy died. They are both in education and both extremely successful with children. Debbie, Kristi and I stay close to Daddy on a regular basis. I know that Mama misses and remembers Daddy all the time, but it seems like my sisters and I still seek or acknowledge contact with him more often than she does.

My life has changed as dramatically as my Mom's, though in a different way. I do believe that I have given control over to God more than I did before. When I remain conscious of that, life seems to flow faster and fuller than before. When I begin to doubt or slow down, I feel the most depressed, or inactive. For the rest of 1995 my massage business boomed. I moved my office into a new building and enjoyed a solo practice. I had my best year financially. Then around Christmas my consciousness started to rumble.

I replayed the last week of Daddy's life on a daily basis, just to keep the facts straight, as I saw them. As I said before, nobody else seemed interested, but I realized the importance of this story to those who want to hear. I heard that a breath workshop was scheduled in February, and after three years of thinking about going, the time had come. I wanted to experience contact with my emotions. Everyone always talked about my anger and told me I had not grieved, and then I watched in awe as Daddy released all his emotions physically, organ by organ, on that Tuesday before his death. I decided then I did not want to wait until my deathbed to start living fully, and I wanted to release anything that held me back now.

I thought the workshop would clear me out, and get me ready to write this book, and continue my work with death and dying. Scared but determined, I went to the Red Lion Hotel on February 8, 1996. Jim agreed to do this with me, and we joined about 100 other eager pioneers. Although I did not look forward to the idea of emoting fully in front of a hundred strangers, I wanted to do whatever God willed. When the music began, I started breathing in earnest. I did not emote. I did have the most beautiful, personal, profound experience with my God that I had ever had. I thought

Daddy's experience was "it." Then I knew integrative breathwork was it, yet I keep having these "its" as time goes on, and I so much want to share them all. Each experience seems more profound than the last, each more spiritually insightful and physically expressed in my being. I write this book, in hopes that this story will jar some folks out of their apathy and disbelief. I want them to realize that God truly exists, that His essence is love, and He will never force Himself on us.

The opposite of God is the absence of God, and if we choose that way, we travel an eternal treadmill. If we throw out everything New Age, we shortchange ourselves on some of the most basic teachings of Jesus Himself. For instance: Just as the Father is in Him, so He is in us and we in Him. Literally, we have all the power He had. If we throw out everything involved with the fundamentalist Christian ethic, we deceive ourselves into believing that evil does not exist. Evil exists, and our minds allow it to have its way. The battle is between our minds and ourselves, not between evil and God.

So with this blessing I invite all of you to listen to the God within you, not to me or anyone else. Then read and pray and listen for the Truth that lights up your heart and soul. I cannot lead you to your path, only that what we think is the way, or the way it should be, isn't always so. You don't have to do workshops constantly, or even meditate on a daily basis; you don't have to go to India or Tibet; you don't have eat only vegetables or abstain from alcohol; you don't have to do anything except acknowledge the existence of God, and then talk to Him like a friend. Most important, listen to what He says to you. Now, I don't devalue anything of those things above. You can use them as tools to help you get in touch a lot quicker. God does not require them of you. I believe God meant for us to experience life. You can have all the knowledge in the world, but if you haven't experienced anything, you haven't learned anything. Live your life everyday, and at the end of each day take time to reflect on what steps you took today that make you feel closer to God. Whom did you love? Whom did you hurt? How does what you did make you feel?

A client talked about heaven and hell versus karma today, and I said that to me they are synonymous in that heaven and hell are the result of karma until we wake up to grace or God, which results in a profound "born again" or "enlightenment" state beyond which there is no return. You can't go back after that.

It's all true! It is literally and even physically all true!

Chapter 13

It's Up to Me

In my dream the angel shrugged and said, 'If we fail this time it will be a failure of imagination. And then she placed the world gently in the palm of my hand..' Brian Andreas

The day after Daddy died, Good Friday, a piece of artwork caught my eye as I walked down the street. I saw a wooden angel, with what looked like bent coat hangers for wings, very modernistic, crudely cut, absent the shape usually attributed to an angel. The words above were printed on it. It spoke to me directly. I had walked by this shop many, many times. I always admired what I saw but I had never bought anything, and never intended to. I don't think I had ever gone inside. I believe my mind still felt altered from the last week, (actually I probably stayed that way for quite a while), and I decided that I had to have that angel. I knew the angel was meant for me. It cost

$172.00. I never spent that kind of money impulsively before. I hadn't worked much the previous six weeks either, but after debating whether I was frivolous or whether I should go home and ask my husband if he minded, I walked in and wrote a check. I owned the angel. Now, I'm sure this same angel has visited the dreams of many, saying the exact same thing. I hope the dreamers listen, because it will take each and every one of us, knowing *that it's up to me*. If we want the world to get better we can't wait for someone else to do it for us. We have to take responsibility for ourselves. God wants us to. He meant for us to. He made us in His image. He imagined us.

I have often thought that when Jesus said, "No one gets to the Father but through *me*," He meant that He couldn't do it for us. We have to say yes and do it for ourselves.

I mentioned earlier in this book that after Daddy died I tried to thank everyone that had helped me develop so far, that allowed me to witness and observe what occurred during Daddy's transition. I felt sure the spiritual teachers I knew would see the implications of my experience. They didn't. Two years later, I began to reach out to other people that talked the talk. They listened to my story, thought the story amazing and that I was sincere, but thought I needed a spiritual director to work in tandem with my therapist, which I didn't have at the time. That doesn't mean I haven't seen a therapist before, but I have almost always used a therapist for a reality check, not as a way of life. I spoke with the director of a seminary here who really seemed to like my story, and even said that he'd always thought he wanted to die quickly, but now he thought he might like to have time to take care of unfinished business. He then said he thought if I wrote a book I should just tell the story and not try to prove any metaphysical ideas. To me the story proves all of the metaphysical ideas, but of course that's me. I know you can't prove that love exists either. This story is a living example of what Jesus taught. Why do churches say the words, and then don't seem to really believe them? Is it just a difference in the levels, or layers, or semantics, or is it because I don't have credentials? People will always listen if you have letters behind your name, or money to back you up, or know somebody that knows somebody. Well, I know God. When you look at what most Christian religions teach, most people didn't even listen to Jesus. If not for the miracles, probably no one would have paid attention. The miracles were not the message, although it's still what preachers preach.

I feel pleased that lay people who ask what I am doing with my time seem really excited about the subject. They often tell me stories of someone witnessing a dying person conversing with a relative or friend from the other side. Several have talked about the dying person wanting to go "home" even when they were home. The word "home" is commonly expressed. Sadly, we don't listen or choose to believe it's true. One person said that her father could not be talking about God or heaven when he mentioned home because "we are Catholics, and Catholics don't talk like that, only Baptists talk like that." I beg to differ. A universal language exists, and many of us don't get to experience it. Consciousness is expanding. Every "me" out there needs to start sharing their stories, letting each other know life is a gift, and we must live every moment. Another friend said that his father kept looking up into the corner and saying, "There's a party and they want me to come," and from my Dad's early experience the week he died, I feel that there probably is quite a party as we make our way back home. Another person said that a widower, in conversation with a new wife, began looking up into the corner. He excused himself to his present wife, and then said, "See you later."

When she questioned him he said, "That was my first wife and she said she'll see me later. Ain't that weird?"

We need to reassure each other that these stories are true. We don't really die, and it's not weird.

I went to church for a noon meditation listed in the bulletin, thinking that if I felt the presence of other people, even one or two, the like minded energy would help me to get the message out. Jesus said, "If two or more or gathered in my name, there I am also."

Three Thursdays in a row and not once did anyone

else come, not even a staff person. The chairs were all set, the leaflets put out, but no people. I stayed and got still. It felt glorious. I still wanted the added energy of others, so I thought maybe Thursday was a bad day, so I went on a Monday. The chairs sat in a circle, but the doors were locked. No human support there.

So God said, "Susan, you can do this, that's my plan." Like the Nike commercial, "Just Do It!"

If God is with me, then who can be against me? Sadly, it's taken me another five years to have the courage in the midst of continuous signs.

God waits on us. I believe it has been fear that has held me back, and as I said earlier, you can't rush the process. I finally love myself, and now it is time.

My thanks to my holy family: my Daddy, my mama, my sisters, my husbands, my children, and all of my friends through the years.

To God be the Glory!

Amen.

Suggested Reading List

I recommend these books to you as my favorites on death & dying and ways to live life. Perhaps you will find them of some help as well.

Final Gifts by Maggie Callanan & Patricia Kelley

Dying Well by Dr. Ira Byock

Saved by the Light by Dannion Brinkley

Denial of the Soul by M. Scott Peck, M.D.

Letters to a Dying Friend by Anton Grosz

The Tibetan Book Of Living and Dying by Sogyal Rinpoche

Living Our Dying A way to the Sacred in Everyday Life by Joseph Sharp

Love, Medicine and Miracles by Dr. Bernie Siegel

Tuesdays With Morrie by Mitch Albom

The Power of Now by Eckhart Tolle

About the Author

Susan Gobin, a fellow traveler on the path, is a spiritual teacher, hospice/Compassion In Action volunteer, and massage therapist. She seeks to share tools that have helped her experience the physical reality of spirituality. She was raised Catholic but now embraces no organized religion, living the Truth inherent in all of them. Her practice is Vipassana meditation as taught by S.N. Goenka.

She offers workshops on stress reduction, meditation and *Self realizing* breathwork to enable a person to experience their true Self. Change and impermanence are the facts of life on a physical and mental level, the universal law of nature or dhamma. Being able to observe this reality, without attachment, is necessary to true happiness. She also acts as a personal consultant on death and dying.

You can reach Susan at Letsallbreathe@aol.com or through her publisher at JNwriter@aol.com. You may write to her c/o *WordWright.biz, Inc.*, P.O. Box 1785, Georgetown, Texas 78627, 512/260-3080.

To order additional copies of
Love is the Healer, Death is a Vehicle

Name ____________________________________

Address __________________________________

____

____

$12.95 x ___________ copies = __________

Sales Tax ____________________
(Texas residents add 8.25% sales tax)

Please add $3.50 postage and handling _______

Total amount due: ___________________________

Please send check or money order for books to:

WordWright.biz, Inc.
P.O. Box 1785
Georgetown, TX 78627

For a complete catalog of books,
visit our site at
http://www.WordWright.biz

Printed in the United States
205512BV00001B/133-237/A